AUTHENTIC TRANSCRIPTIONS
WITH NOTES AND TABLATURE

Start Something

2 We Still Kill The Old Way

13 To Hell We Ride

23 LAST TRAIN HOME

33 Make A Move

40 Burn, Burn

50 I Don't Know

61 HELLO AGAIN

68 GOODBYE TONIGHT

76 Start Something

83 A Million Miles

92 Last Summer

101 SWAY

109 Guitar Notation Legend

Music transcriptions by Addi Booth and David Stocker

ISBN 0-634-08370-8

HAL•LEONARD®
CORPORATION
7777 W. BLUEMOUND RD. P.O. BOX 13819 MILWAUKEE, WI 53213

In Australia Contact:
Hal Leonard Australia Pty. Ltd.
22 Taunton Drive P.O. Box 5130
Cheltenham East, 3192 Victoria, Australia
Email: ausadmin@halleonard.com

Visit Hal Leonard Online at
www.halleonard.com

We Still Kill the Old Way

Words and Music by Michael Lewis, Ian Watkins, Richard Oliver, Lee Gaze, Stuart Richardson and Michael Chiplin

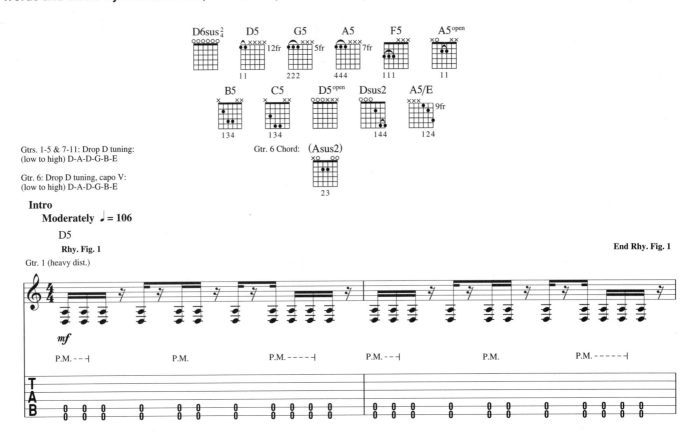

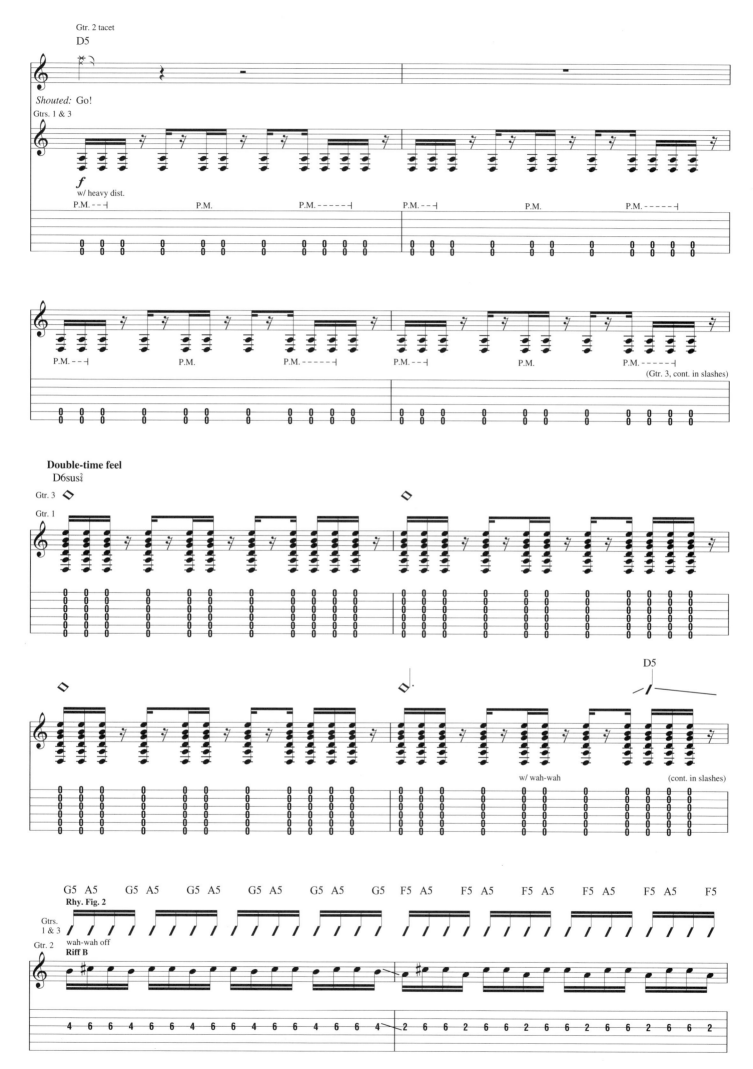

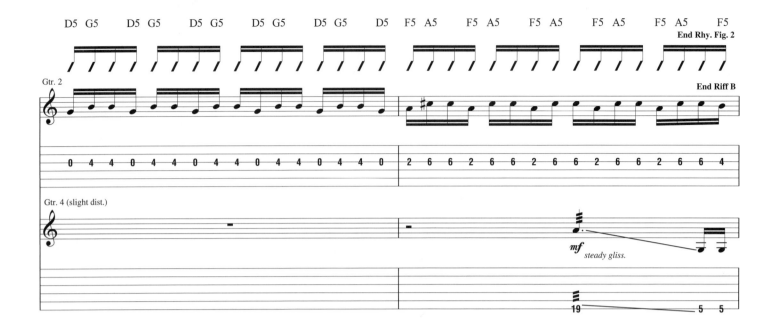

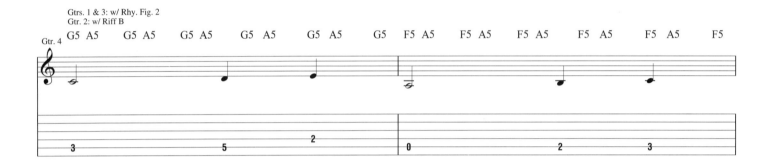

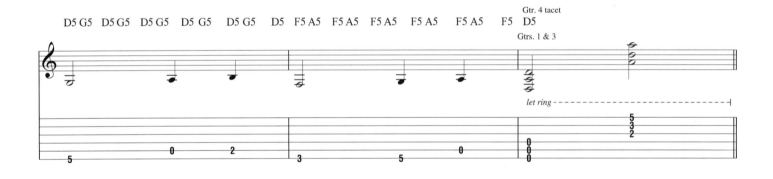

Verse

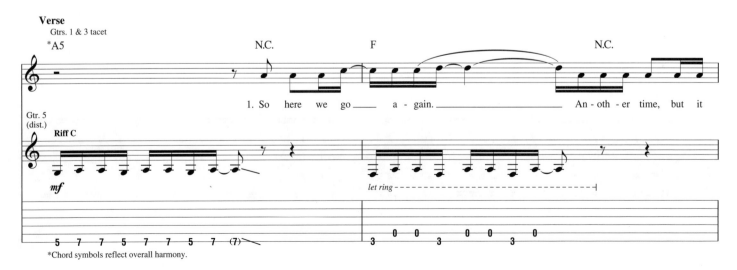

*Chord symbols reflect overall harmony.

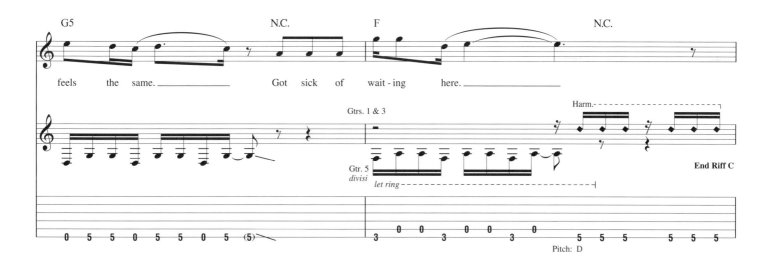

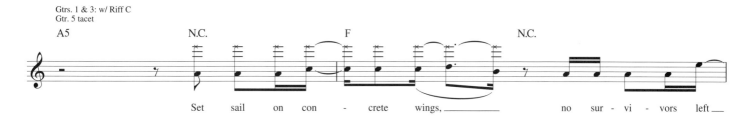

Pre-Chorus

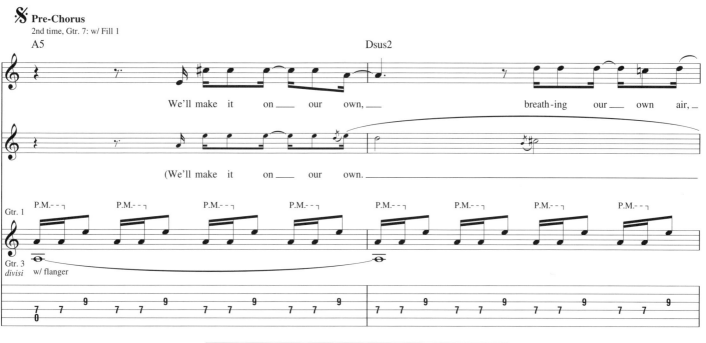

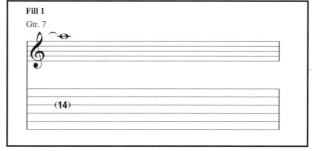

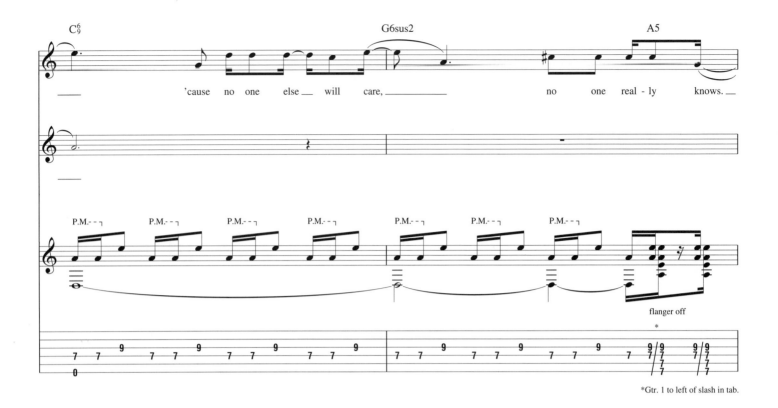

'cause no one else ___ will care, _____ no one real - ly knows. ___

flanger off

*Gtr. 1 to left of slash in tab.

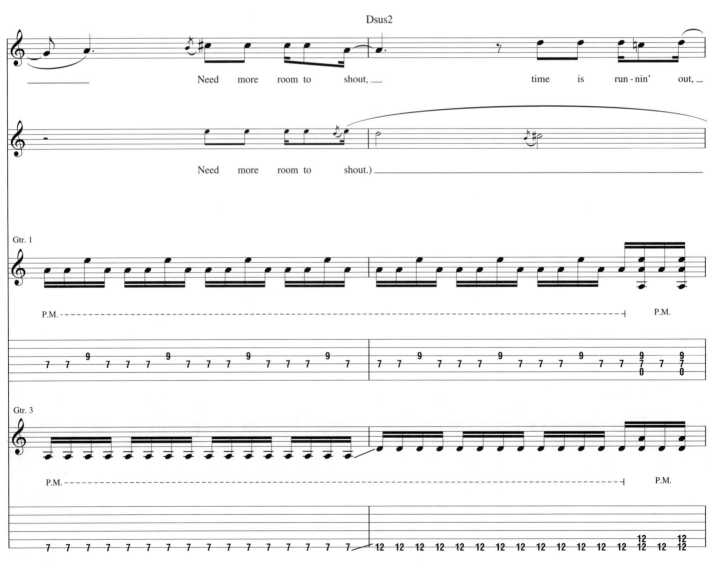

Need more room to shout, ___ time is run - nin' out, ___

Need more room to shout.) _____

Gtr. 1

P.M. -| P.M.

Gtr. 3

P.M. -| P.M.

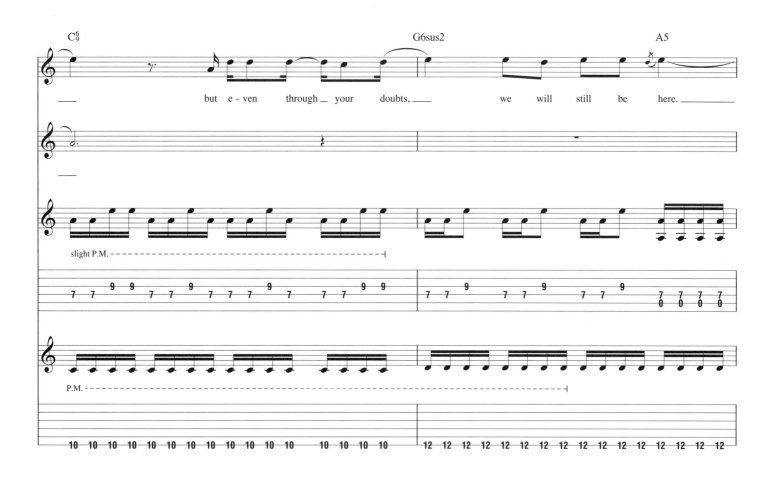

but e-ven through__ your doubts,___ we will still be here._____

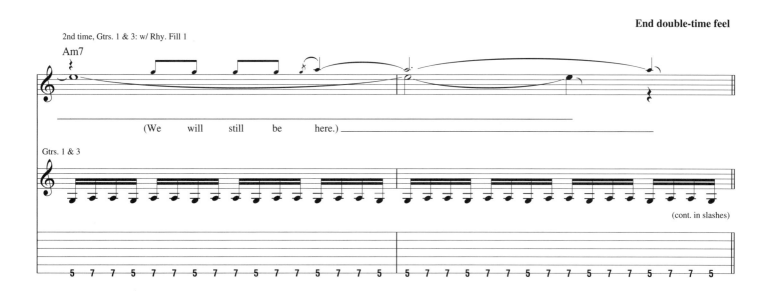

End double-time feel

2nd time, Gtrs. 1 & 3: w/ Rhy. Fill 1

Am7

(We will still be here.)_____

Gtrs. 1 & 3

(cont. in slashes)

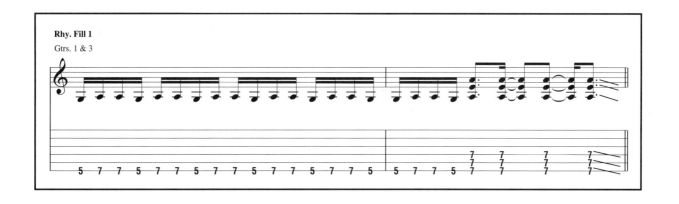

Rhy. Fill 1

Gtrs. 1 & 3

Chorus

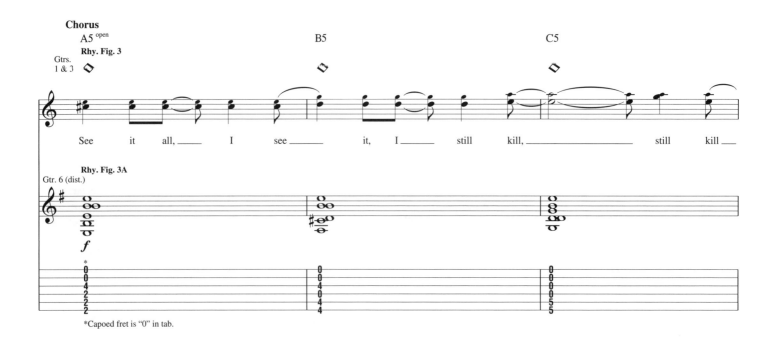

See it all,___ I see___ it, I___ still kill,___ still kill

*Capoed fret is "0" in tab.

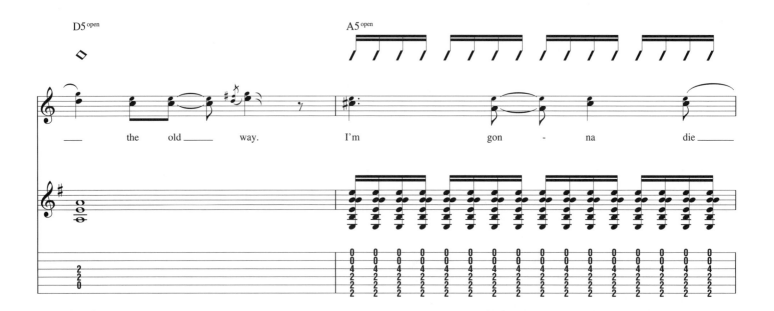

___ the old___ way. I'm gon - na die___

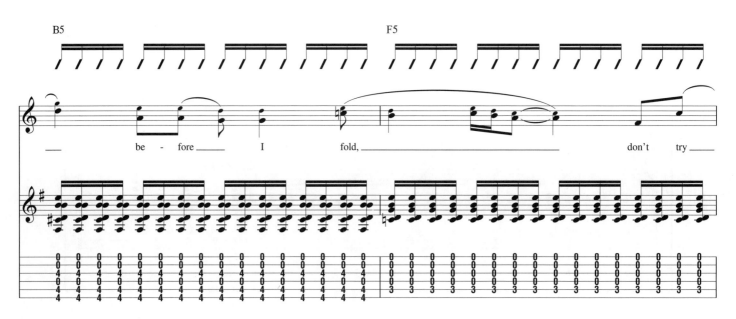

___ be - fore___ I fold,___ don't try___

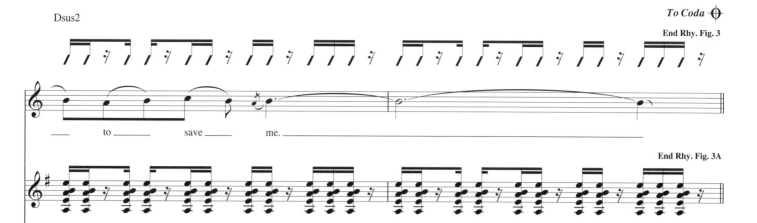

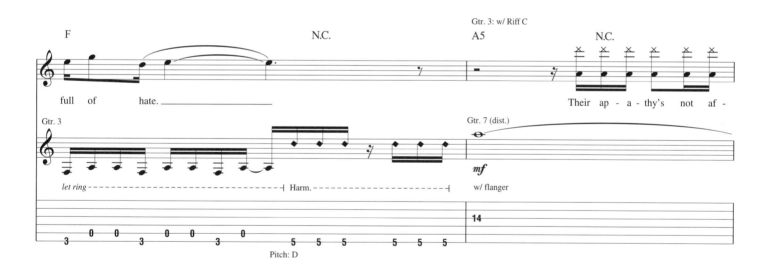

Coda

Interlude

Gtrs. 1 & 3: w/ Rhy. Fig. 1 (2 times)
Gtr. 6 tacet

Gtr. 2: w/ Riff A

D5

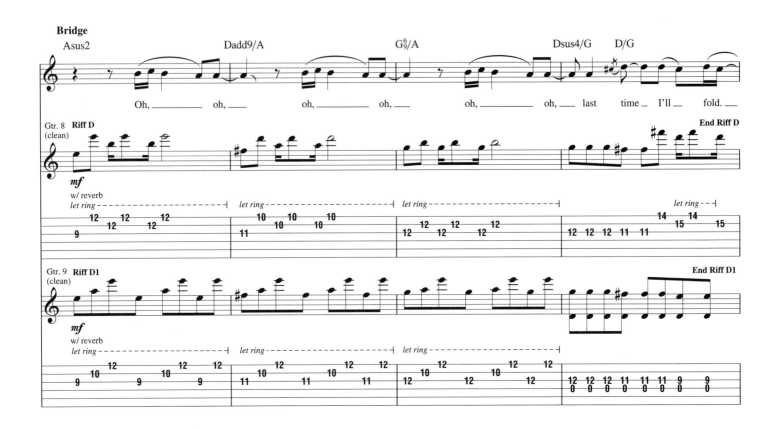

Bridge

Asus2   Dadd9/A   G⁶₉/A   Dsus4/G   D/G

Oh, ___ oh, ___ oh, ___ oh, ___ oh, ___ oh, last time _ I'll _ fold.

Gtr. 8 **Riff D**
(clean)

End Riff D

mf
w/ reverb
let ring

Gtr. 9 **Riff D1**
(clean)

End Riff D1

mf
w/ reverb
let ring

Gtrs. 8 & 9: w/ Riffs D & D1

Asus2   Dadd9/A   G⁶₉/A   Dsus4/G   D/G

___ Oh, ___ oh, ___ oh, ___ oh, ___ this is the last time _ I'll _ fold. ___

Gtrs. 8 & 9 tacet

Chorus

A5/E

N.C.(A5)

Gtrs.
8 & 9

See it all, ___ I see ___

Gtr. 10
(dist.)

mf
let ring

10

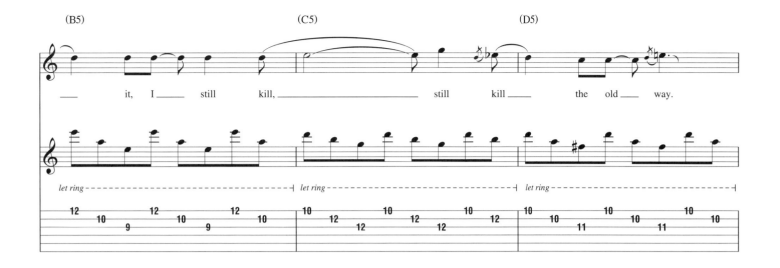

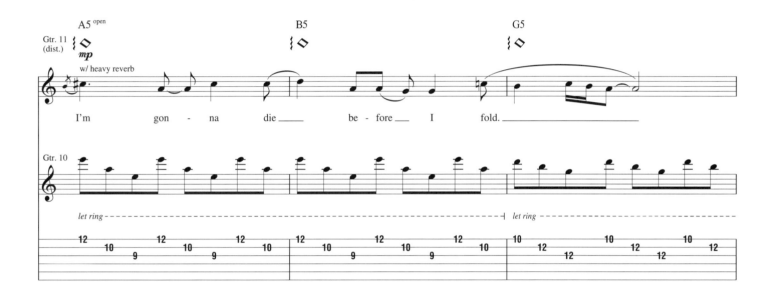

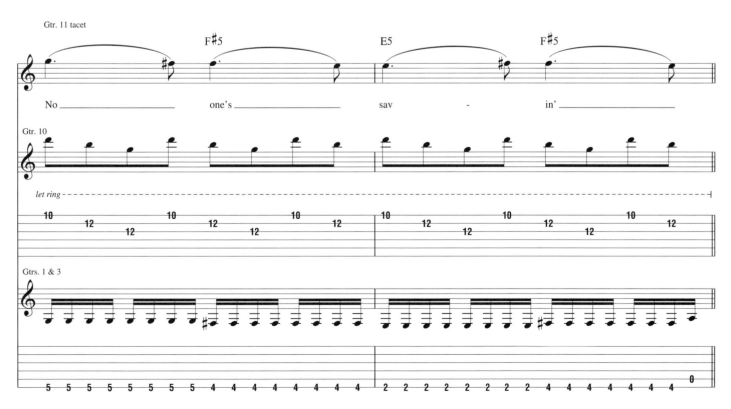

Chorus

Gtrs. 1 & 3: w/ Rhy. Fig. 3
Gtr. 6: w/ Rhy. Fig. 3A
Gtr. 10 tacet

A5
*(E5)

B13sus4
(F#13sus4)

C
(G)

D5
(A5)

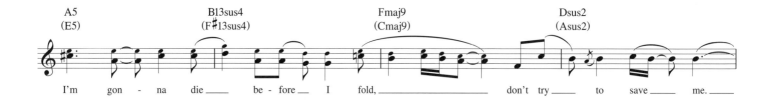

See it all,___ I see___ it, I___ still kill,_____ still kill___ the old___ way.

me.___

*Chord symbols in parentheses represent chord names respective to capoed guitar.
Symbols above represent actual sounding chords.

A5
(E5)

B13sus4
(F#13sus4)

Fmaj9
(Cmaj9)

Dsus2
(Asus2)

I'm gon - na die___ be - fore I fold,_____ don't try___ to save___ me.___

Outro

Gtrs. 3 & 6 tacet

(Asus2)

D5

Gtr. 6

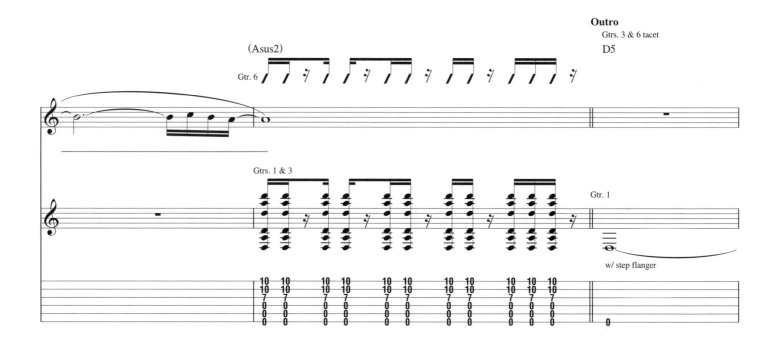

Gtrs. 1 & 3

Gtr. 1

w/ step flanger

Segue to "To Hell We Ride"

N.C.

Gtr. 1

(Drums & live audience) **4**

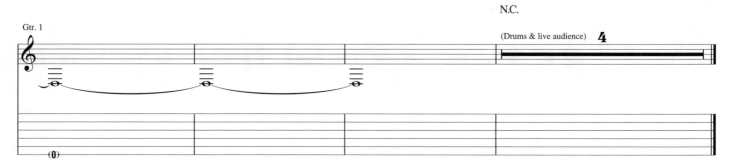

To Hell We Ride

Words and Music by Michael Lewis, Ian Watkins, Richard Oliver, Lee Gaze, Stuart Richardson and Michael Chiplin

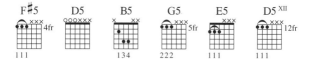

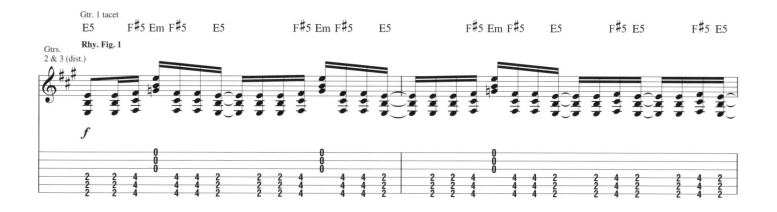

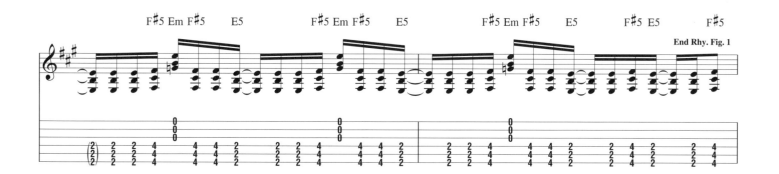

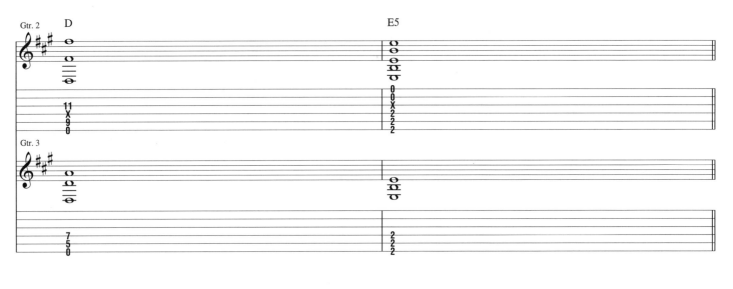

Verse

Double-time feel

1. With you it's nev-er good ___ e-nough, ___ be-cause you

Riff A

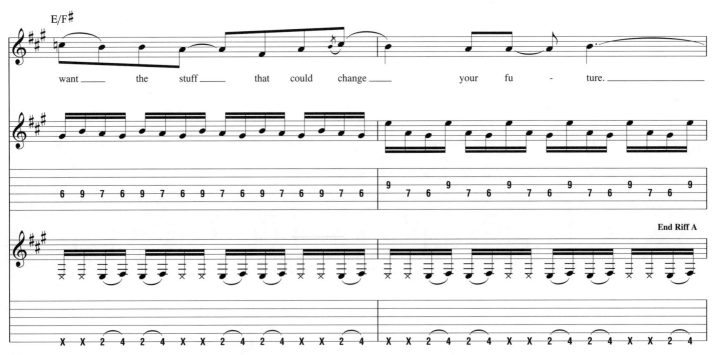

want ___ the stuff ___ that could change ___ your fu - ture. ___

End Riff A

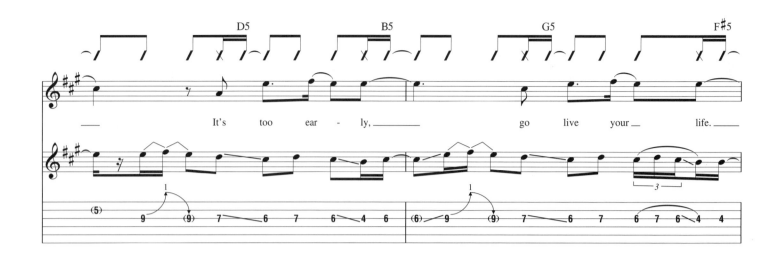

It's too ear-ly, _____ go live your ___ life. _____

End double-time feel

1st time Gtr. 3 tacet
2nd time, Gtr. 3: w/ Rhy. Fill 1
Gtr. 4 tacet

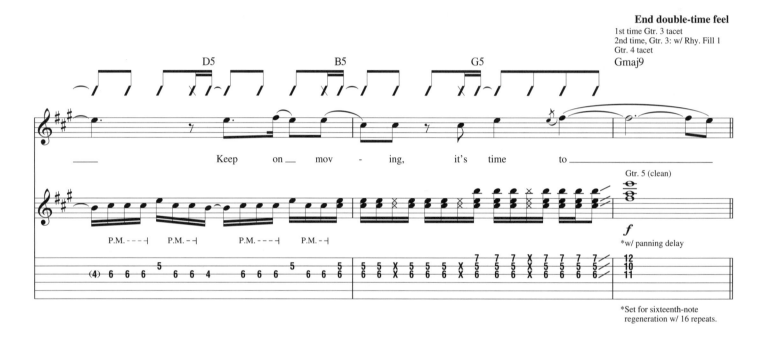

Keep on ___ mov - ing, it's time to _____

Gtr. 5 (clean)

*w/ panning delay

*Set for sixteenth-note
regeneration w/ 16 repeats.

Chorus

**Gtrs. 2 & 3: w/ Rhy. Fig. 1
Gtr. 5 tacet

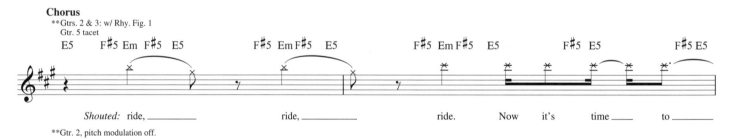

Shouted: ride, _____ ride, _____ ride. Now it's time ___ to ___

**Gtr. 2, pitch modulation off.

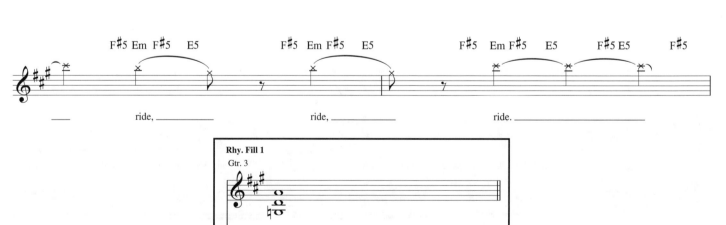

ride, _____ ride, _____ ride.

Rhy. Fill 1

Gtr. 3

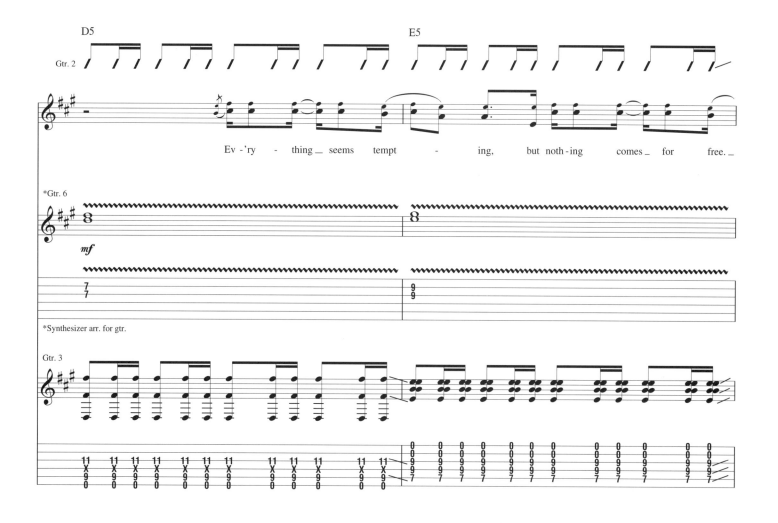

Ev -'ry - thing __ seems tempt - ing, but noth-ing comes __ for free. __

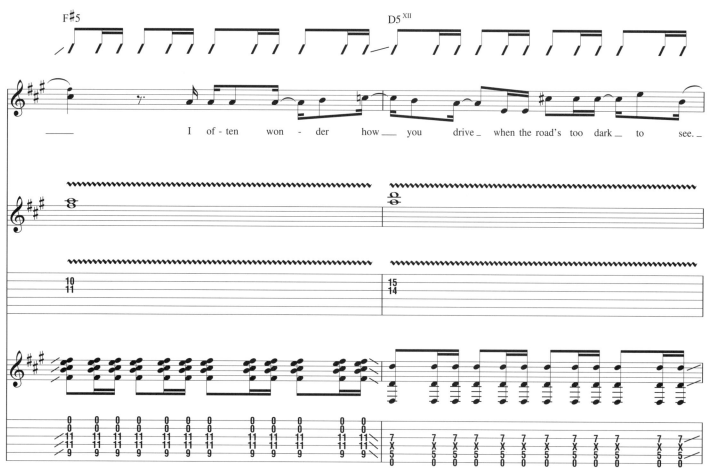

__ I of-ten won - der how __ you drive __ when the road's too dark __ to see. __

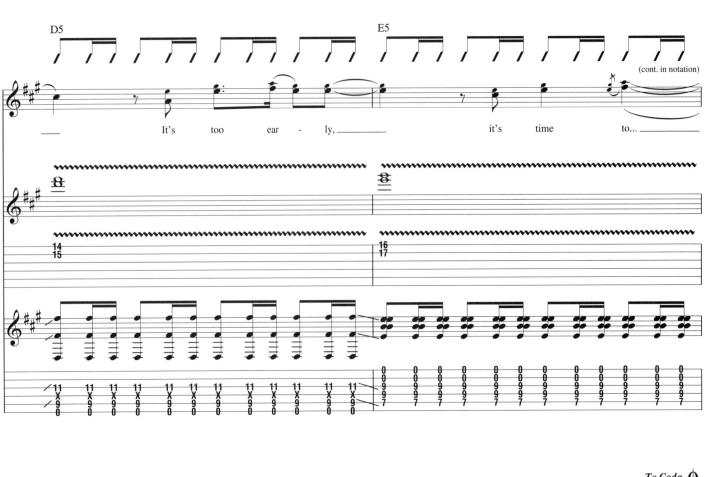

It's too ear - ly, _____ it's time to... _____

Shouted: ride, _____ ride, _____ ride. _____

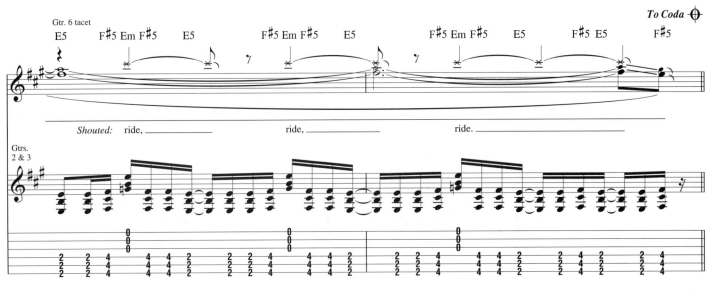

Verse
Double-time feel
Gtr. 3: w/ Riff A (2 times)

2. We light the fire to watch_ it burn,_ but when it comes_ your turn,_ all that's left _____ is em - bers._

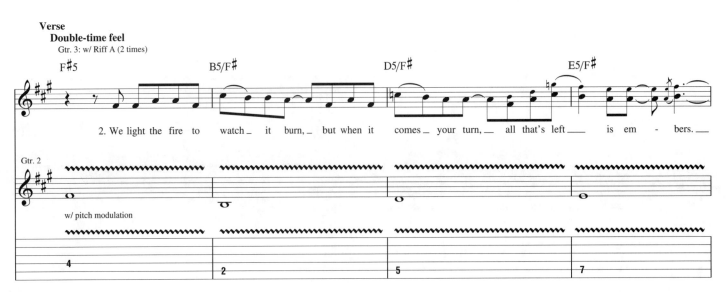

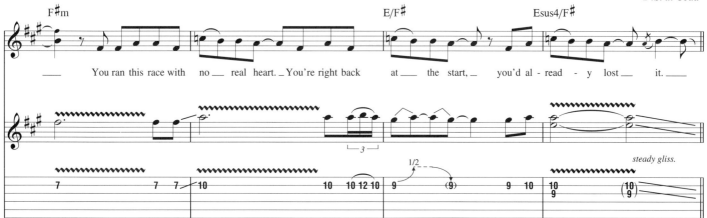

Coda

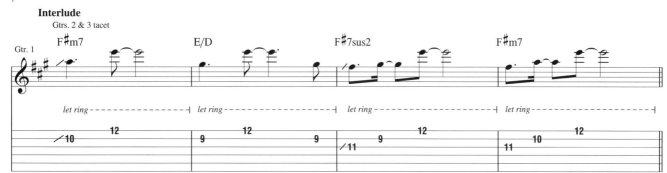

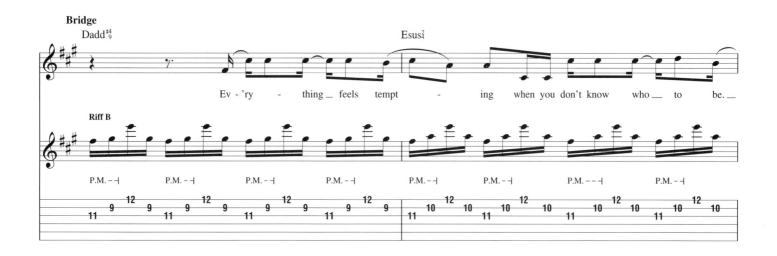

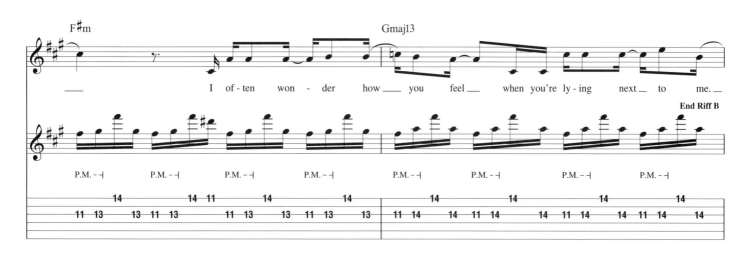

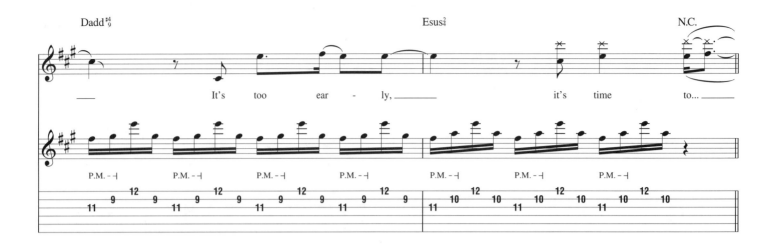

It's too ear - ly, _____ it's time to... _____

Interlude

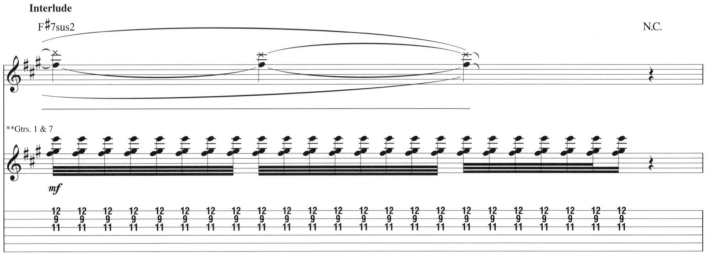

**Gtrs. 1 & 7

mf

**Gtr. 7 w/ dist. Gtr. 1: flanger & wah-wah off.

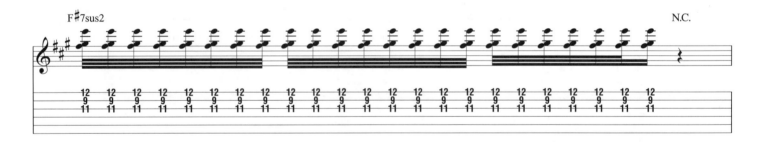

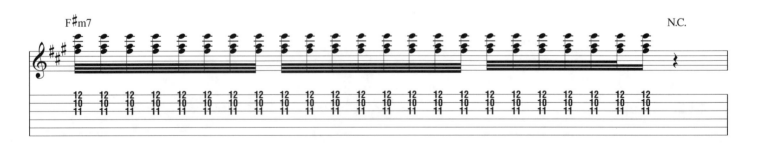

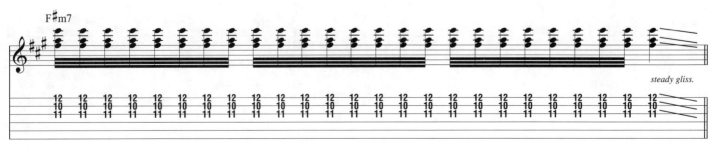

steady gliss.

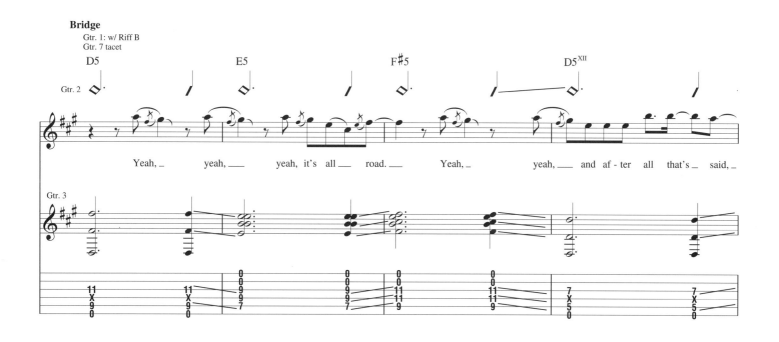

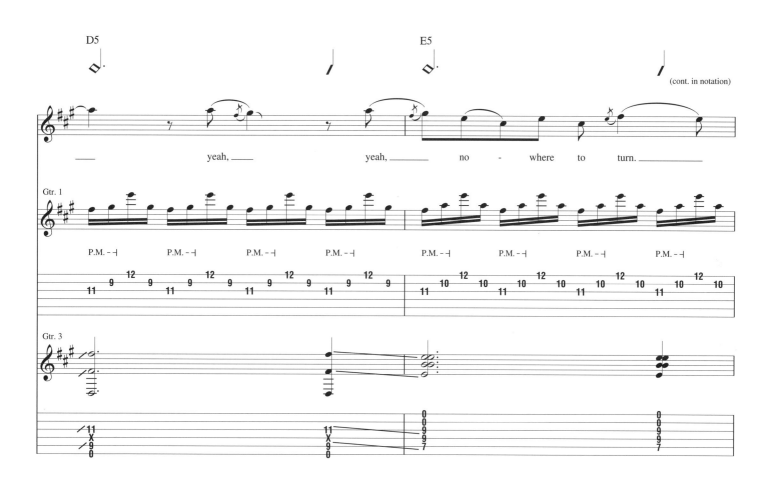

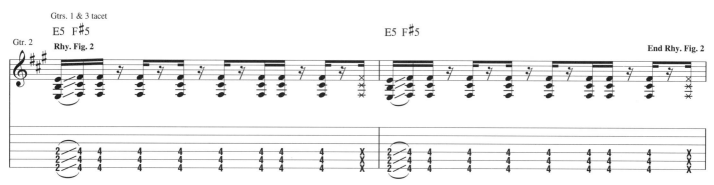

Last Train Home

Words and Music by Michael Lewis, Ian Watkins, Richard Oliver, Lee Gaze, Stuart Richardson and Michael Chiplin

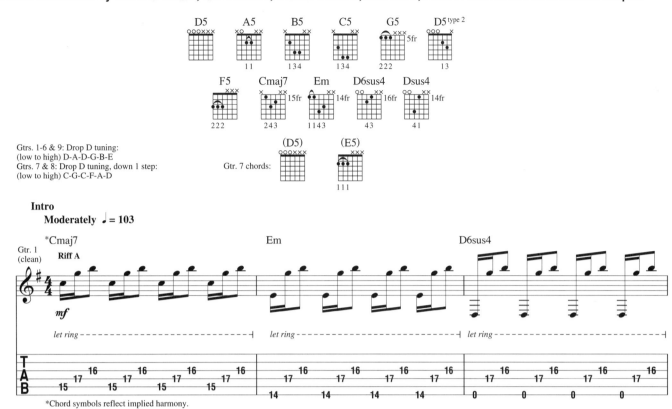

Gtrs. 1-6 & 9: Drop D tuning:
(low to high) D-A-D-G-B-E
Gtrs. 7 & 8: Drop D tuning, down 1 step:
(low to high) C-G-C-F-A-D

Gtr. 7 chords:

Intro

Moderately ♩ = 103

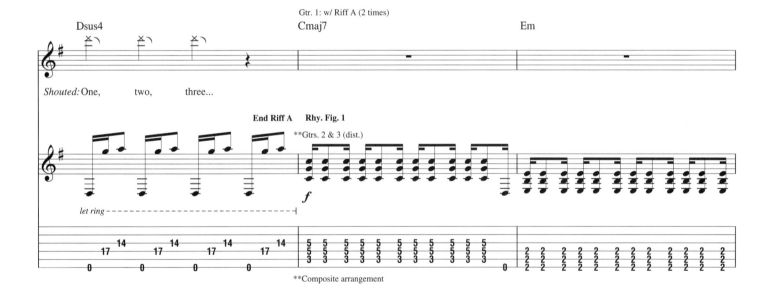

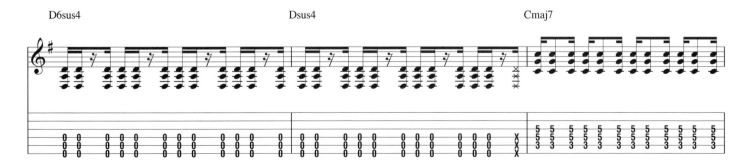

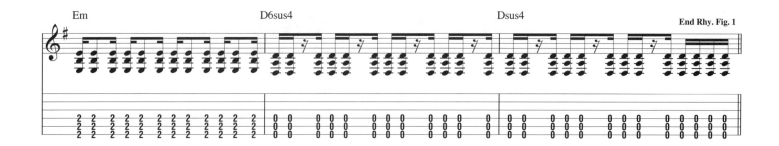

Verse

Gtrs. 2 & 3 tacet

1. To ev-'ry bro - ken heart ___ in here, ___

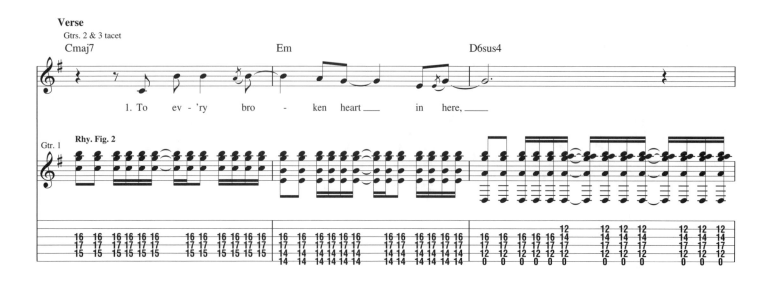

love ___ was once ___ a part, ___ but now ___

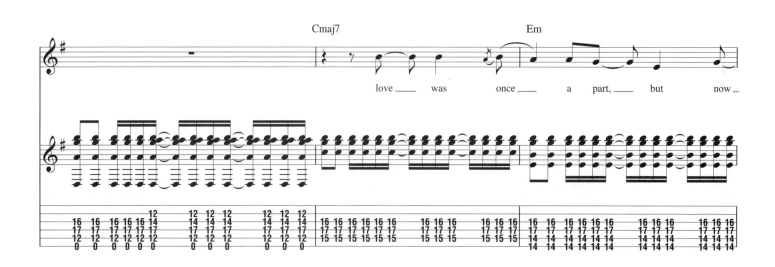

___ it's ___ dis - ap - peared. ___ She told me that it's

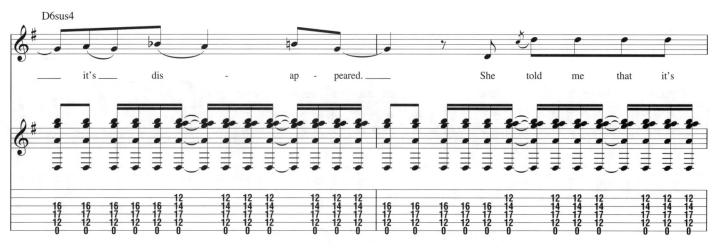

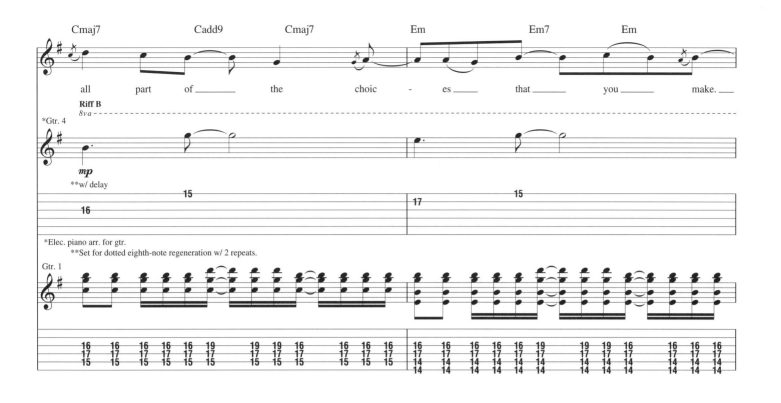

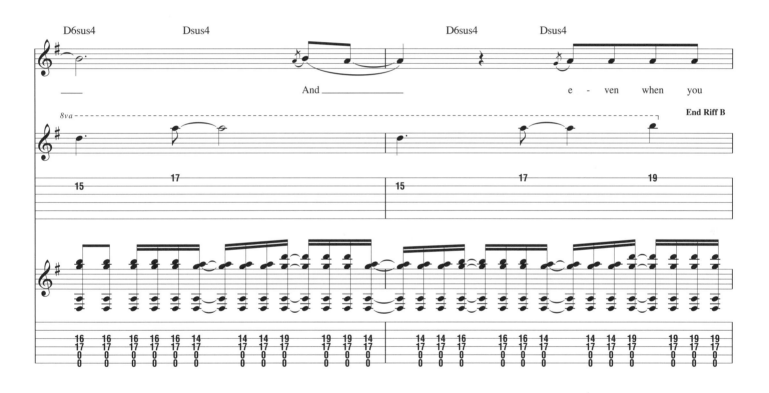

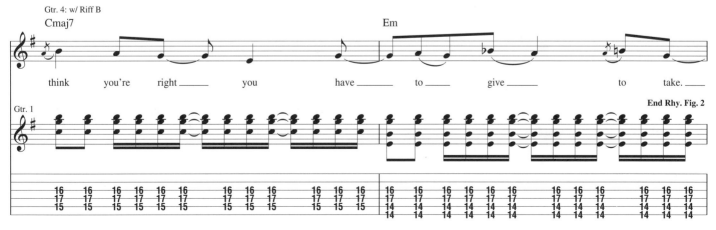

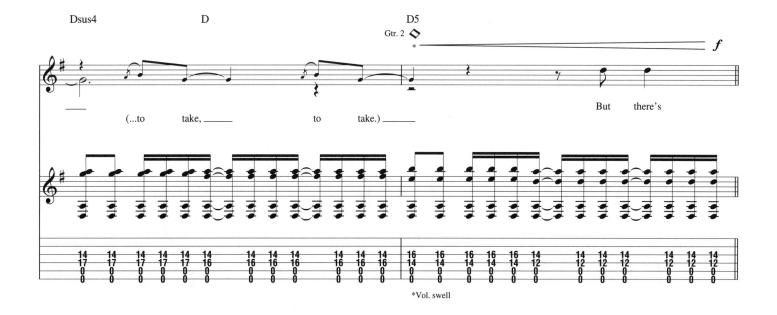

*Vol. swell

𝄋 Pre-Chorus
Double-time feel
Gtrs. 1 & 4 tacet

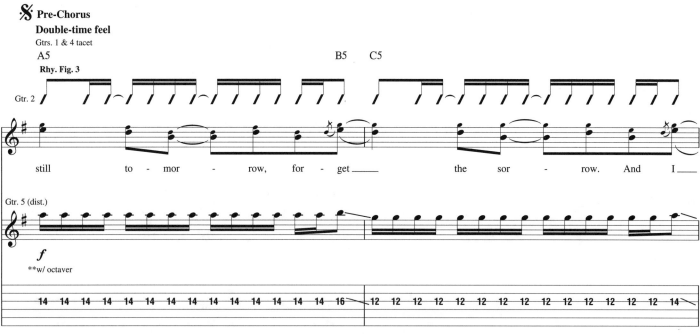

**Set for one octave above.

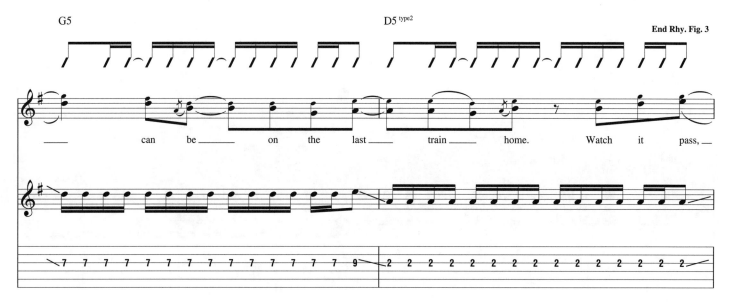

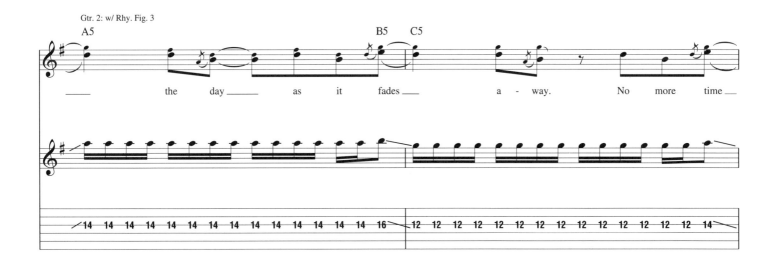

End double-time feel

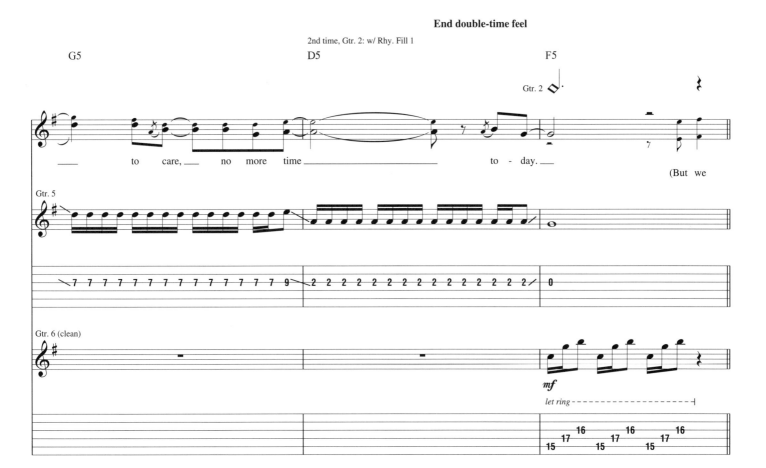

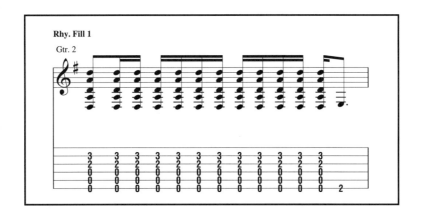

1st time, Gtr. 1: w/ Riff A (2 times)
1st time, Gtrs. 2 & 3: w/ Rhy. Fig. 1
2nd time, Gtr. 1: w/ Riff A (1 3/4 times)
2nd time, Gtrs. 2 & 3: w/ Rhy. Fig. 1 (1st 7 meas.)
Gtrs. 5 & 6 tacet

If we're go-ing no - where, ___ if it's not e - nough. ___

Voc. Fig. 1

sing, ___ yeah, we sing, ___ and we

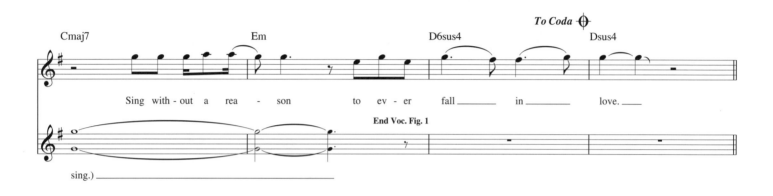

To Coda

Sing with-out a rea - son to ev - er fall ___ in ___ love. ___

End Voc. Fig. 1

sing.) ___

Verse

Gtr. 1: w/ Rhy Fig. 2

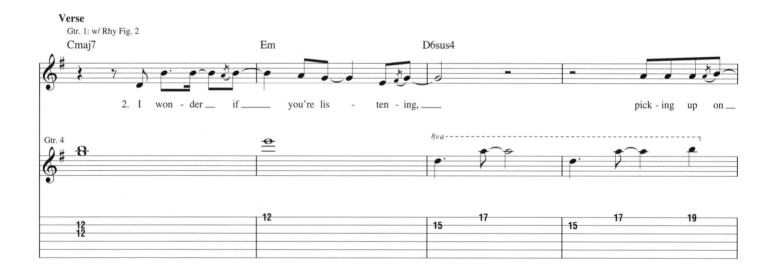

2. I won - der ___ if ___ you're lis - ten - ing, ___ pick - ing up on ___

Gtr. 4

8va

Gtr. 4: w/ Riff B (2 3/4 times)

___ the sig - nals sent ___ back ___ with - in.

Some-times it feels like I don't real - ly know ___ what's go - ing ___ on.

Time and time a - gain it seems __ like ev - 'ry - thing __ is __

D.S. al Coda

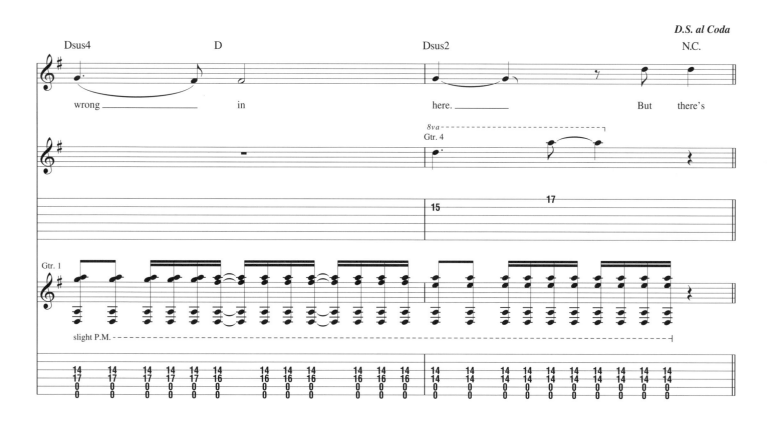

wrong __ in here. __ But there's

Coda

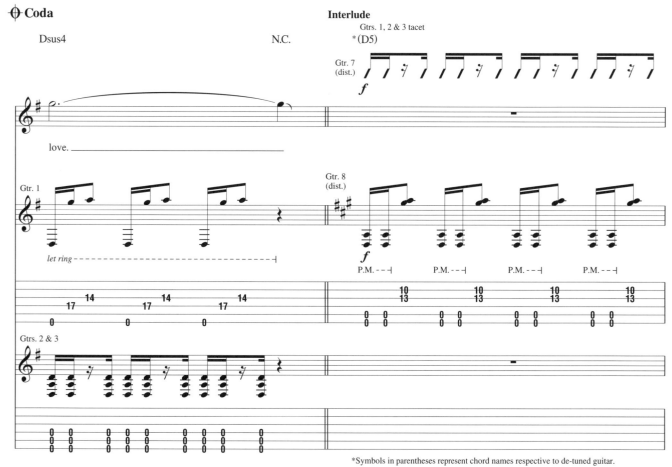

love. __

*Symbols in parentheses represent chord names respective to de-tuned guitar.

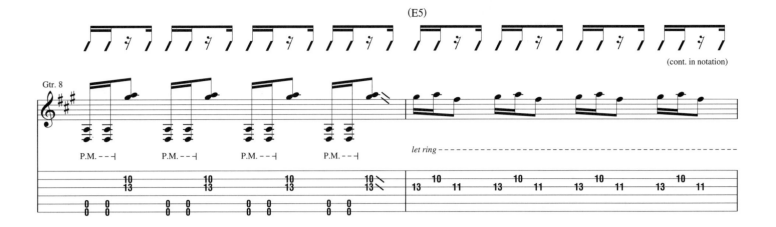

(cont. in notation)

Chorus

Dadd⁴⁄₂
*(Eadd⁴⁄₂)

Cmaj7
(Dmaj7)

But   we   sing   if   we're   go - in'   no -

*Symbols in parentheses represent chord names respective to de-tuned guitar. Symbols above represent actual sounding chords.

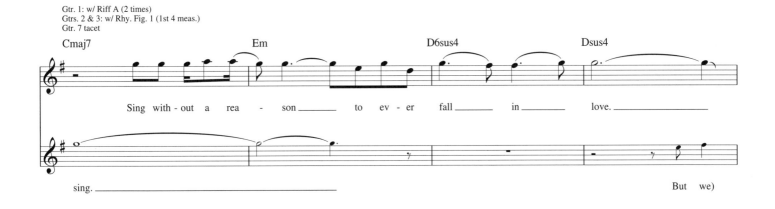

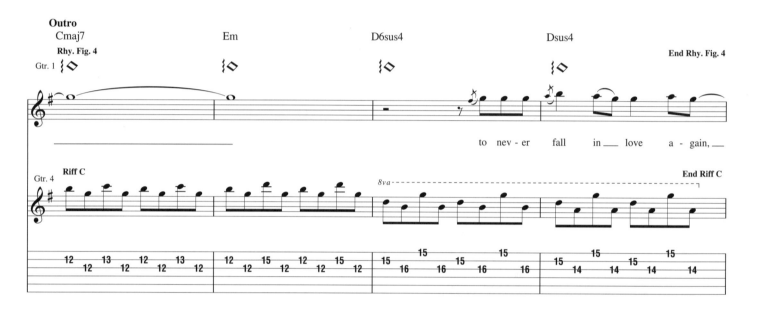

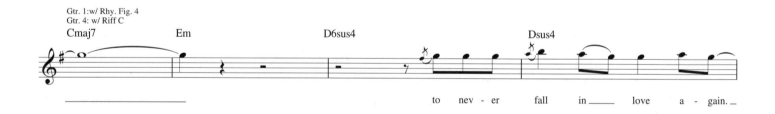

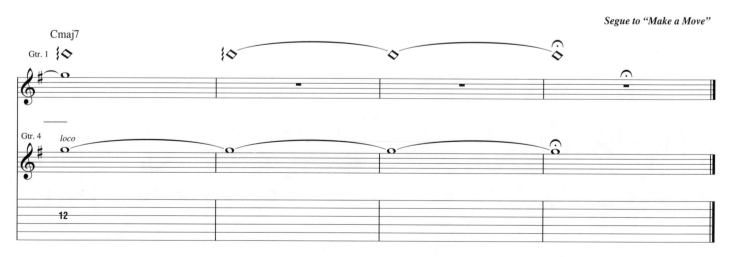

Make a Move

Words and Music by Michael Lewis, Ian Watkins, Richard Oliver, Lee Gaze, Stuart Richardson and Michael Chiplin

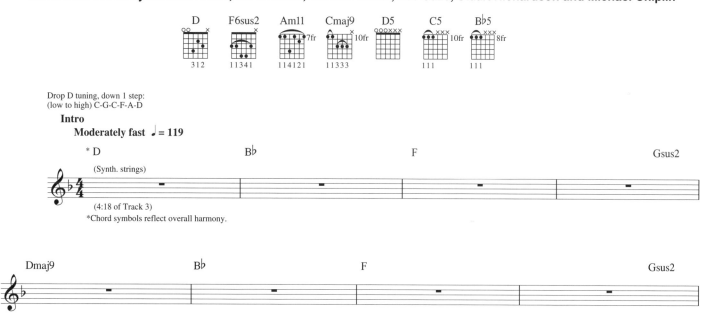

Drop D tuning, down 1 step:
(low to high) C-G-C-F-A-D

Intro

Moderately fast ♩ = 119

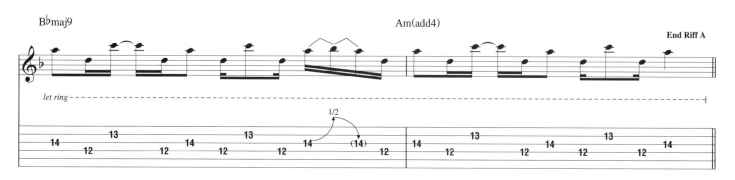

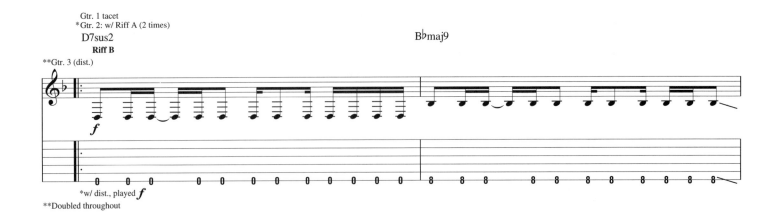

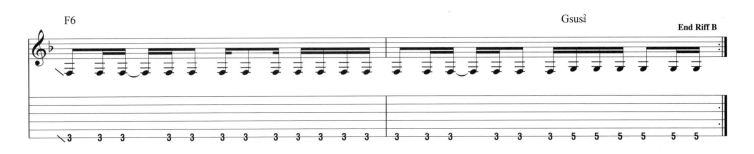

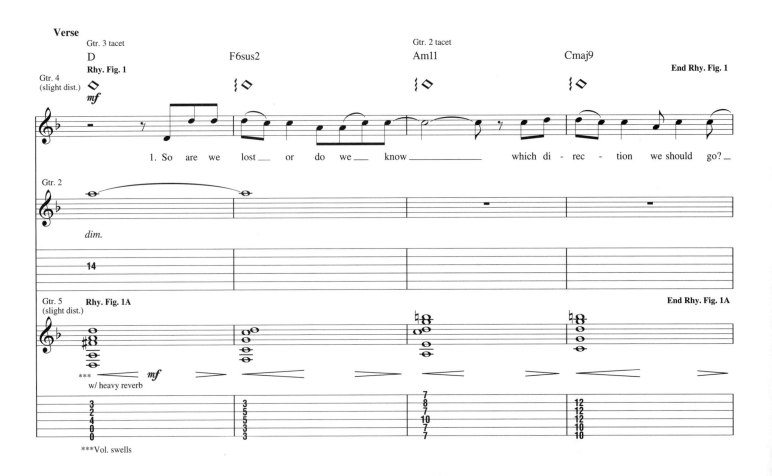

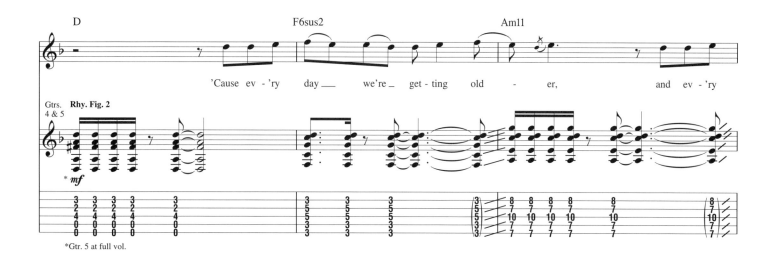

'Cause ev-'ry day ___ we're ___ get-ting old - er, and ev-'ry

Gtrs. **Rhy. Fig. 2**
4 & 5

* *mf*

*Gtr. 5 at full vol.

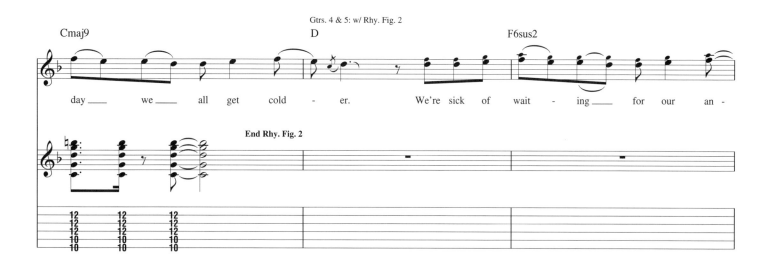

Gtrs. 4 & 5: w/ Rhy. Fig. 2

day ___ we ___ all get cold - er. We're sick of wait - ing ___ for our an -

End Rhy. Fig. 2

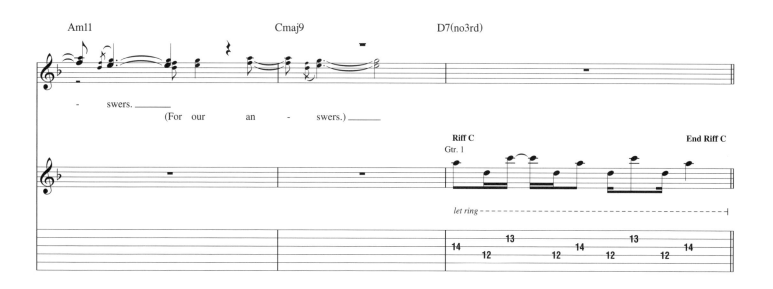

- swers. ___ (For our an - swers.) ___

Riff C
Gtr. 1

End Riff C

let ring -

Chorus
Gtr. 1 tacet
Gtr. 3: w/ Riff B (2 times)

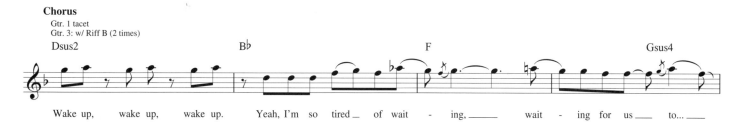

Wake up, wake up, wake up. Yeah, I'm so tired ___ of wait - ing, ___ wait - ing for us ___ to...

Wake up, wake up, wake up. Yeah, I'm so sick of ___ wait - ing ___ for us ___

Verse
Gtr. 5: w/ Rhy. Fig. 1A (2 times)

___ to ___ make ___ a ___ move. ___ 2. Are we meant ___ to take the bait? ___

___ Should we sit ___ a - round and wait? ___ Are we

be - in' saved, or was that an - oth - er lie ___ you made ___ to make ___ us hate?

*w/ echo set
as before.

Gtrs. 4 & 5: w/ Rhy. Fig. 2 (2 times)

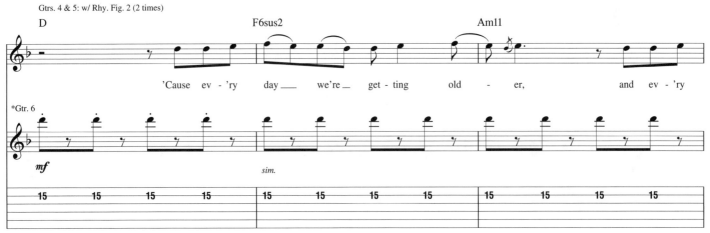

'Cause ev - 'ry day ___ we're ___ get - ting old - er, and ev - 'ry

*Gtr. 6

mf   *sim.*

*Strings arr. for gtr.

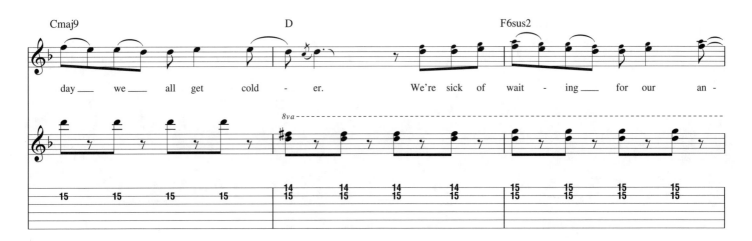

day ___ we ___ all get cold - er. We're sick of wait - ing ___ for our an -

8va

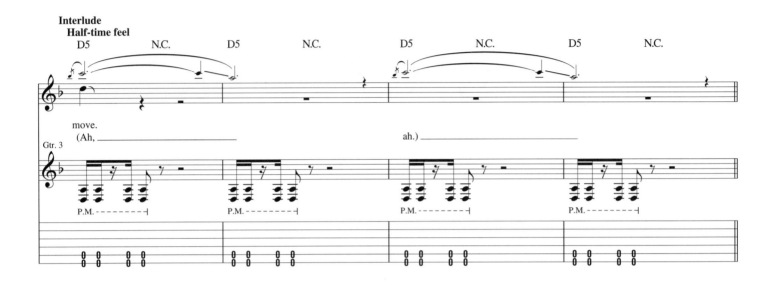

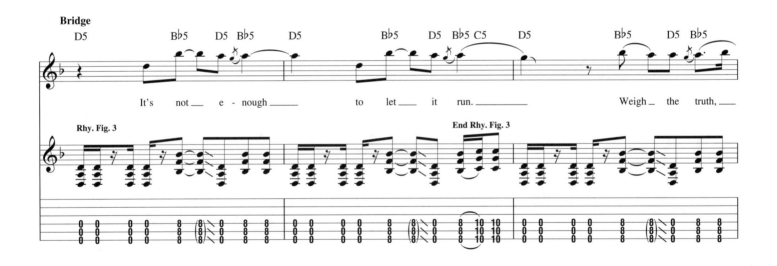

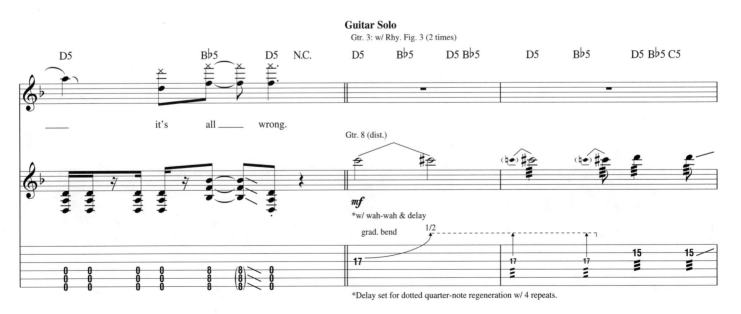

*Delay set for dotted quarter-note regeneration w/ 4 repeats.

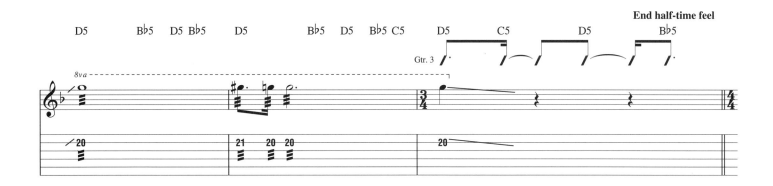

Bridge

D.S. al Coda

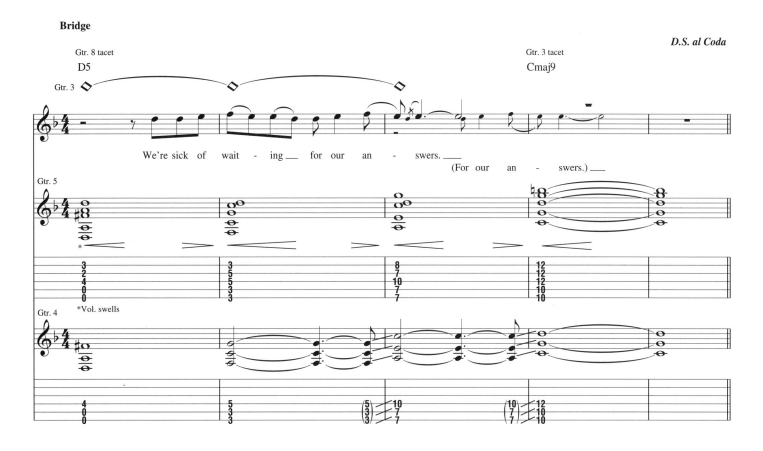

We're sick of wait - ing ___ for our an - swers. ___

(For our an - swers.) ___

Segue to "Burn, Burn"

⊕ Coda
Outro

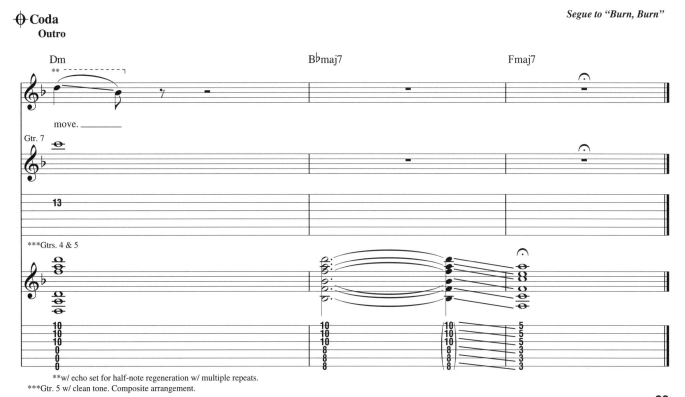

move. ___

**w/ echo set for half-note regeneration w/ multiple repeats.
***Gtr. 5 w/ clean tone. Composite arrangement.

Burn, Burn

Words and Music by Michael Lewis, Ian Watkins, Richard Oliver, Lee Gaze, Stuart Richardson and Michael Chiplin

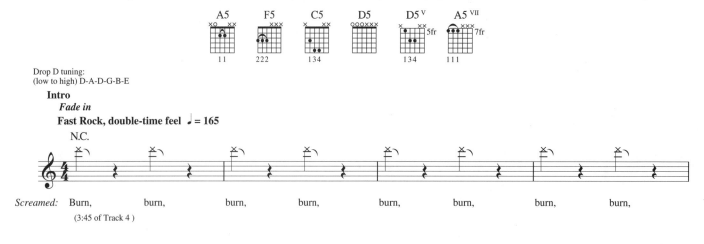

Drop D tuning:
(low to high) D-A-D-G-B-E

Intro
Fade in
Fast Rock, double-time feel ♩ = 165

N.C.

Screamed: Burn,   burn,   burn,   burn,   burn,   burn,   burn,   burn,

(3:45 of Track 4)

End double-time feel

burn,   burn,   burn,   burn,   yeah!

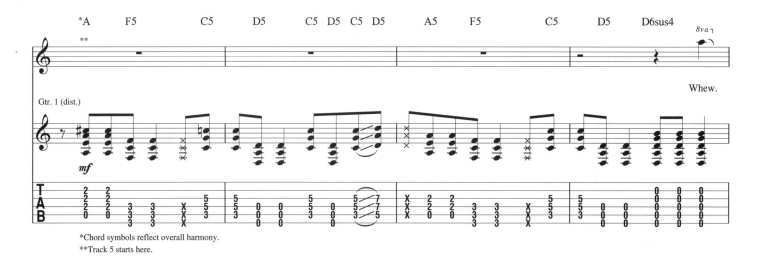

*Chord symbols reflect overall harmony.
**Track 5 starts here.

**Composite arrangement

***Harmonic located approximately 1/3 the
distance between the 2nd & 3rd frets.

Pitch: D

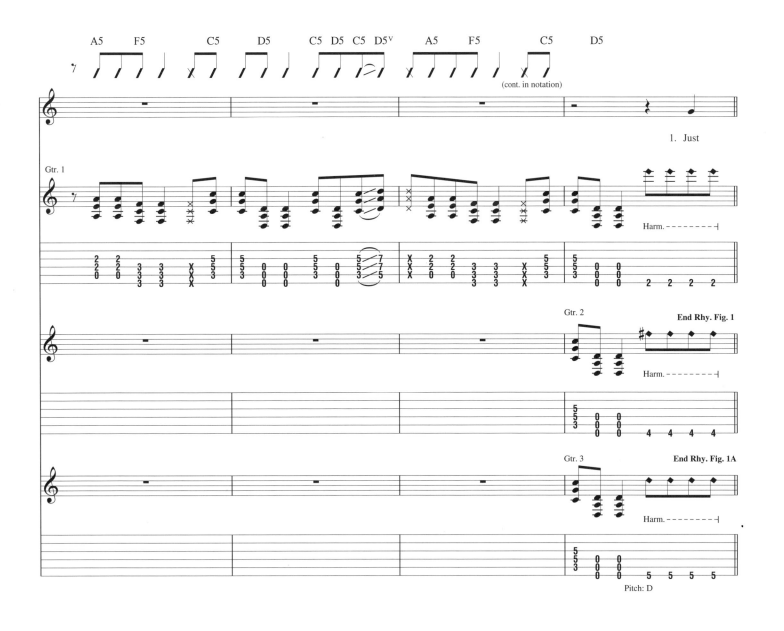

Verse

where do I be-gin with this life we're liv - ing in? Mar-

- ket youth their u - ni - form, make us all fit in. But do you think

Chorus

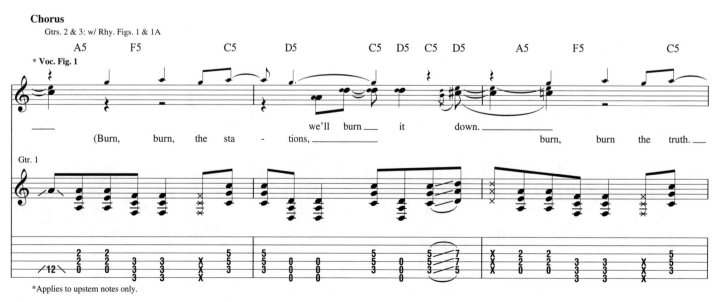

*Applies to upstem notes only.

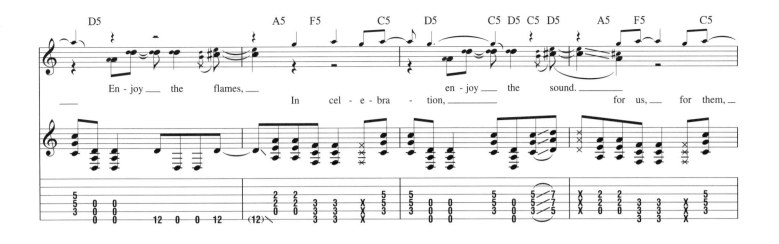

Verse

Gtr. 1 tacet

*Bass arr. for gtr.
**Chords implied by bass, next 16 meas.

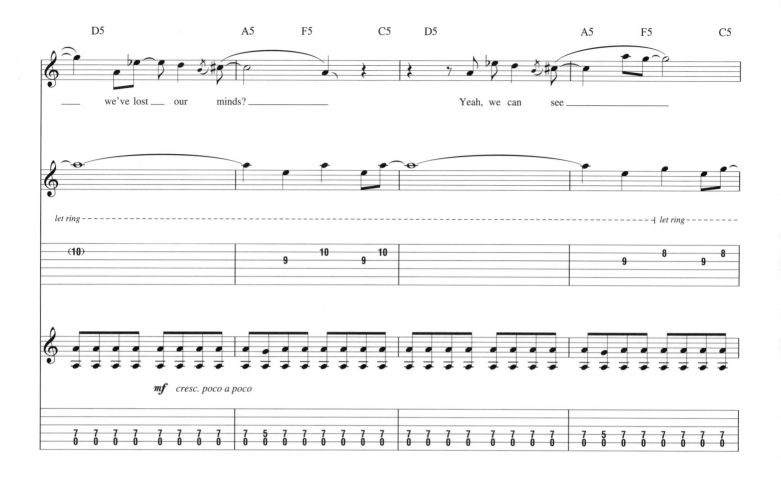

we've lost ___ our ___ minds? _____ Yeah, we can ___ see ___

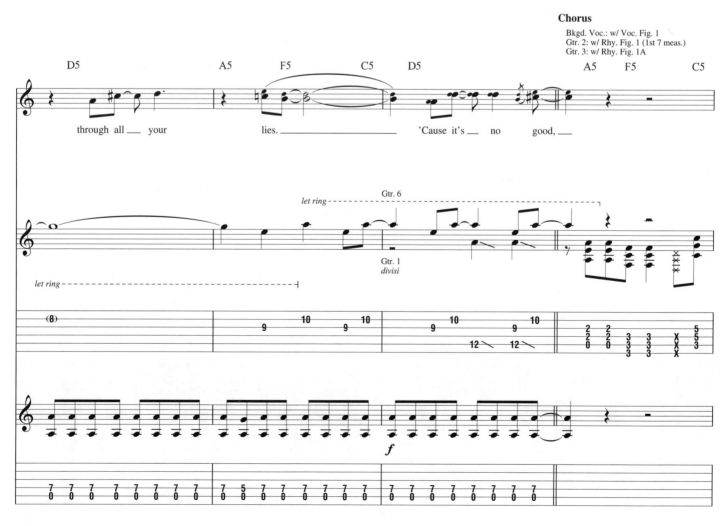

through all ___ your ___ lies. _____ 'Cause it's ___ no ___ good, ___

Chorus
Bkgd. Voc.: w/ Voc. Fig. 1
Gtr. 2: w/ Rhy. Fig. 1 (1st 7 meas.)
Gtr. 3: w/ Rhy. Fig. 1A

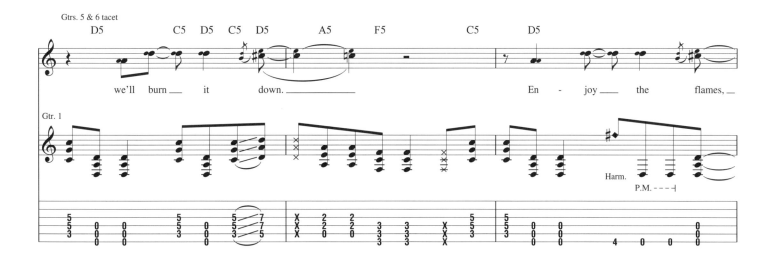

we'll burn ___ it down. ___ En - joy ___ the flames, ___

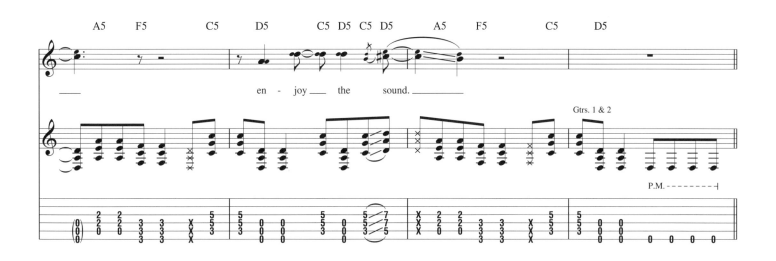

___ en - joy ___ the sound. ___

Interlude

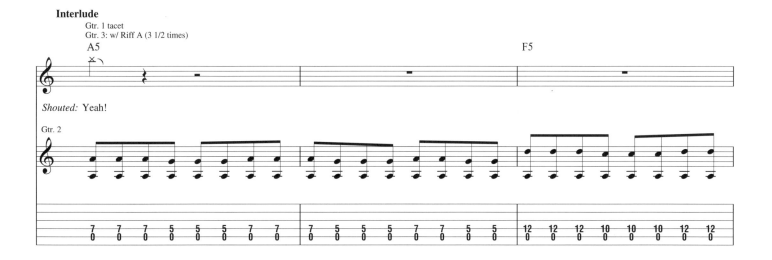

Shouted: Yeah!

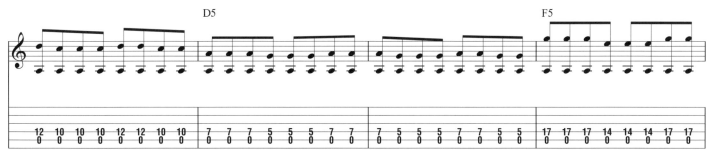

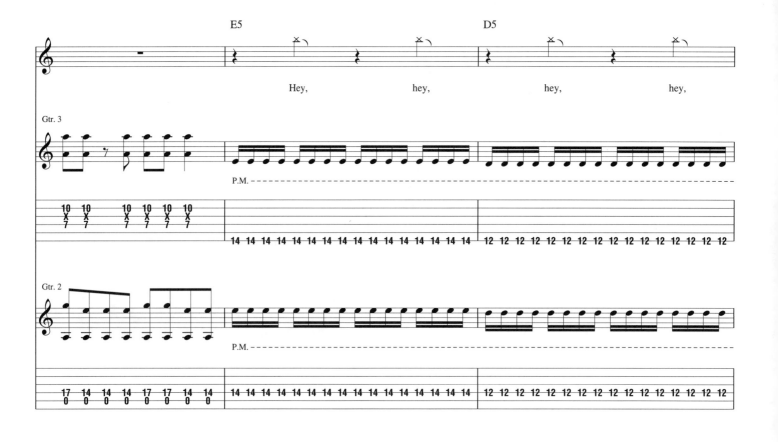

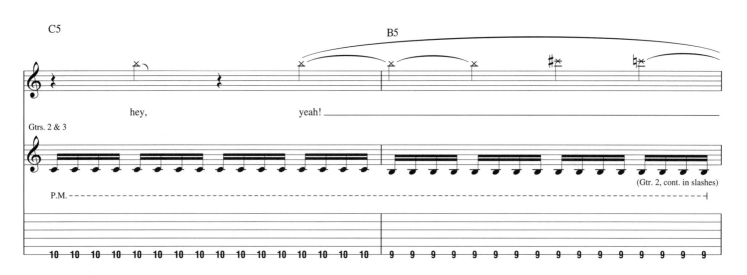

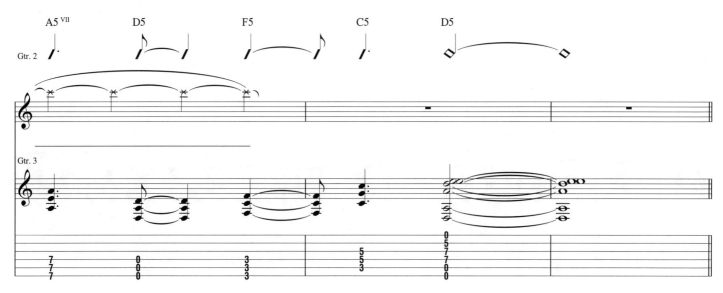

Bridge

Gtr. 2 tacet
Gtr. 3: w/ Riff A (7 1/2 times)

w/ random michrophonic fdbk. (next 15 meas.)

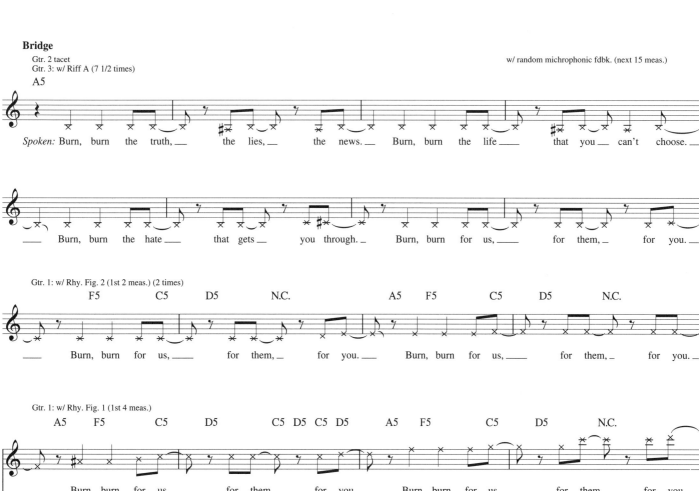

Spoken: Burn, burn the truth, ___ the lies, ___ the news. ___ Burn, burn the life ___ that you ___ can't choose. ___

___ Burn, burn the hate ___ that gets ___ you through. ___ Burn, burn for us, ___ for them, ___ for you. ___

Gtr. 1: w/ Rhy. Fig. 2 (1st 2 meas.) (2 times)

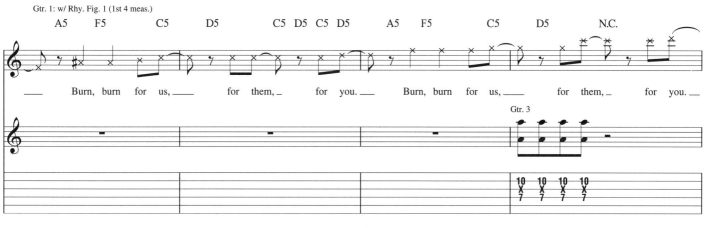

___ Burn, burn for us, ___ for them, ___ for you. ___ Burn, burn for us, ___ for them, ___ for you. ___

Gtr. 1: w/ Rhy. Fig. 1 (1st 4 meas.)

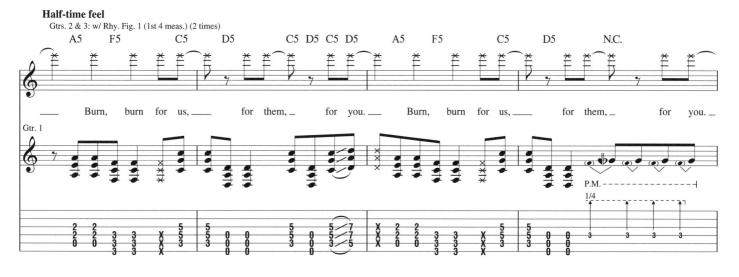

___ Burn, burn for us, ___ for them, ___ for you. ___ Burn, burn for us, ___ for them, ___ for you. ___

Half-time feel

Gtrs. 2 & 3: w/ Rhy. Fig. 1 (1st 4 meas.) (2 times)

End half-time feel

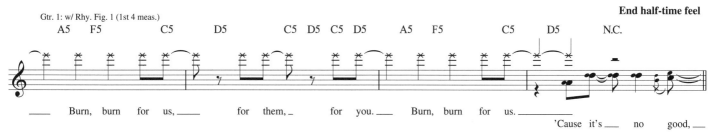

___ Burn, burn for us, ___ for them, ___ for you. ___ Burn, burn for us, ___ for them, ___ for you. ___

Gtr. 1: w/ Rhy. Fig. 1 (1st 4 meas.)

___ Burn, burn for us, ___ for them, ___ for you. ___ Burn, burn for us. ___

'Cause it's ___ no good, ___

Chorus

Bkgd. Voc.: w/ Voc. Fig. 1 (2 times)
Gtr. 2: w/ Rhy. Fig. 1
Gtr. 3: w/ Rhy. Fig. 1A (1st 7 meas.)

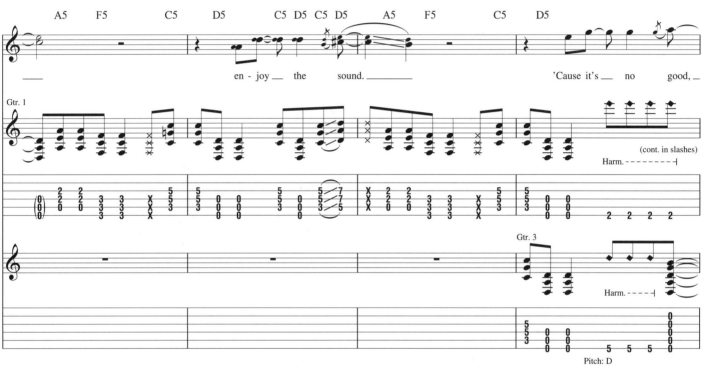

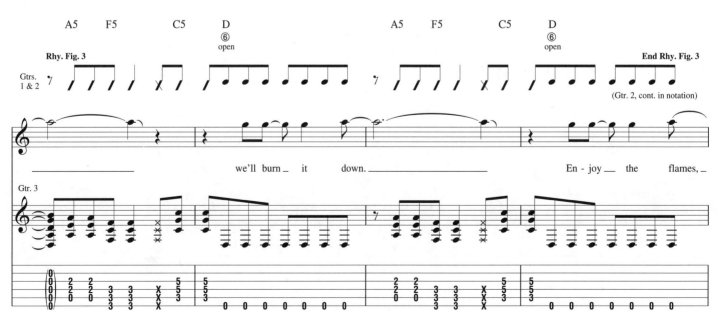

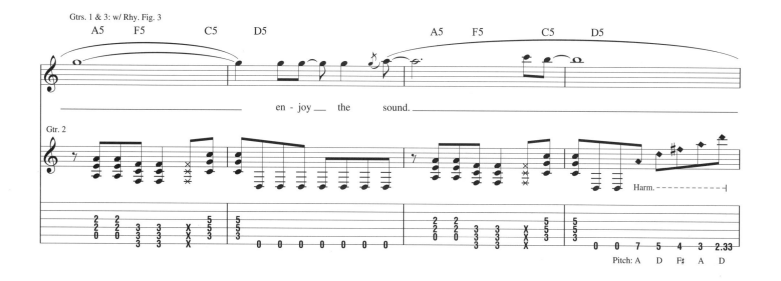

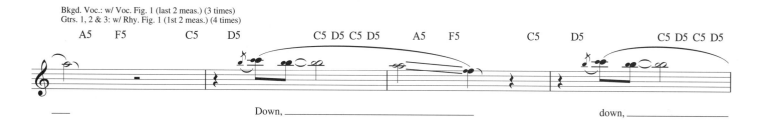

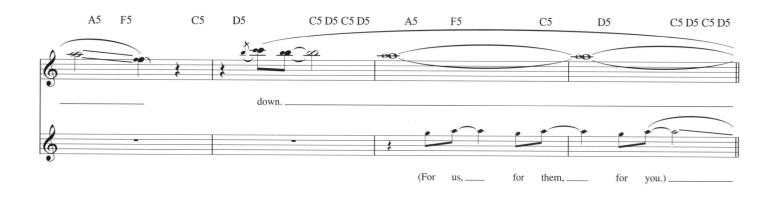

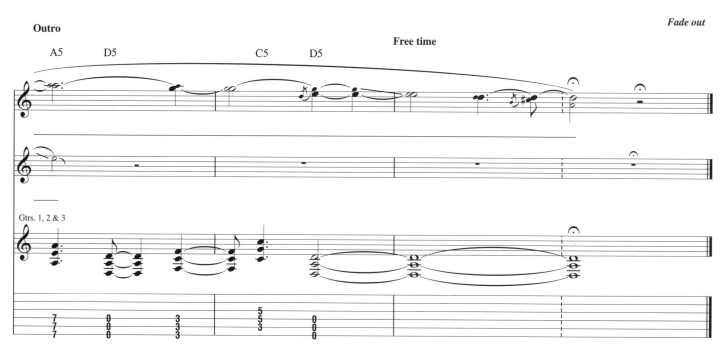

I Don't Know

Words and Music by Michael Lewis, Ian Watkins, Richard Oliver, Lee Gaze, Stuart Richardson and Michael Chiplin

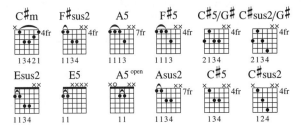

Drop D tuning:
(low to high) D-A-D-G-B-E

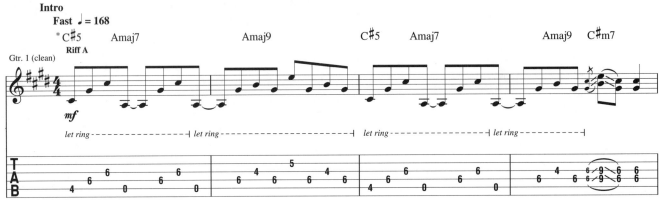

*Chord symbols reflect basic harmony.

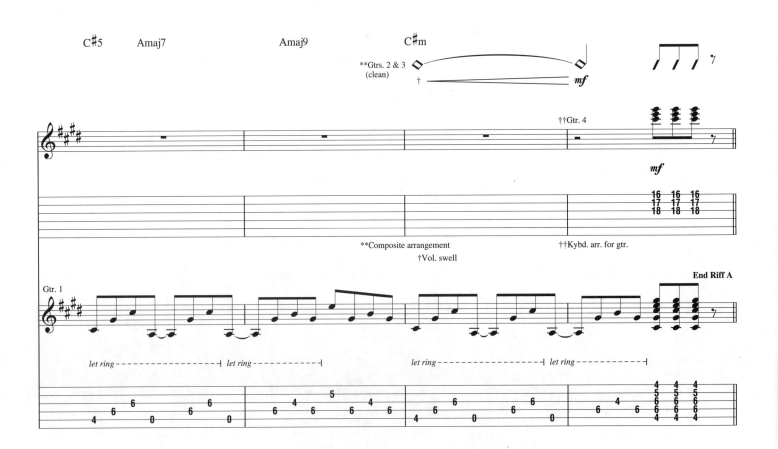

**Composite arrangement   ††Kybd. arr. for gtr.
†Vol. swell

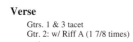

Verse

Gtrs. 1 & 3 tacet
Gtr. 2: w/ Riff A (1 7/8 times)

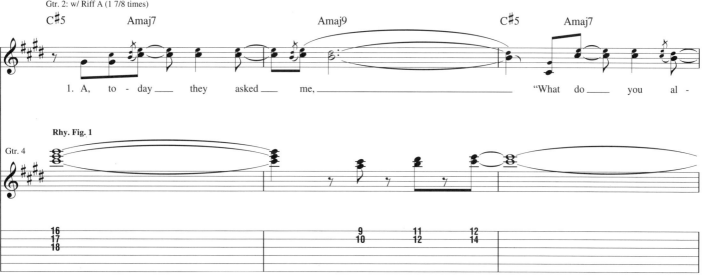

1. A, to - day ___ they asked ___ me, ___ "What do ___ you al -

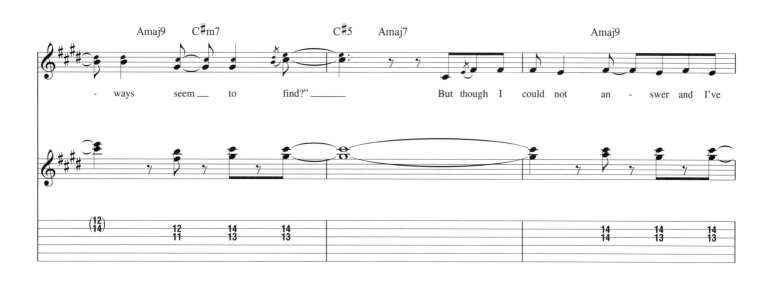

- ways seem ___ to find?" ___ But though I could not an - swer and I've

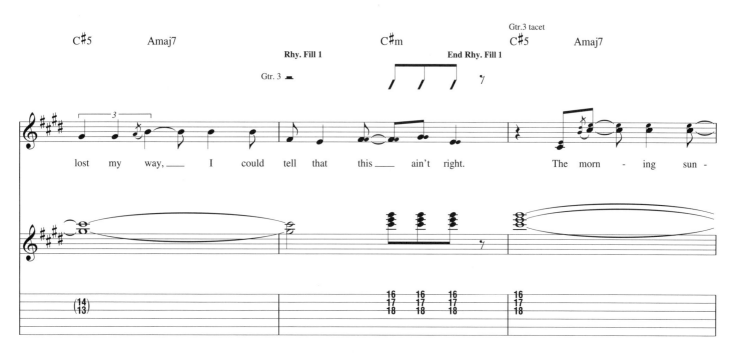

lost my way, ___ I could tell that this ___ ain't right. The morn - ing sun -

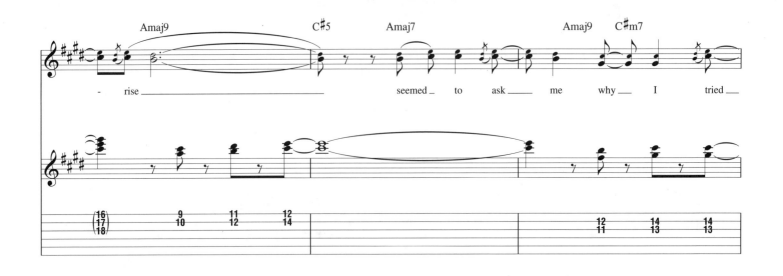

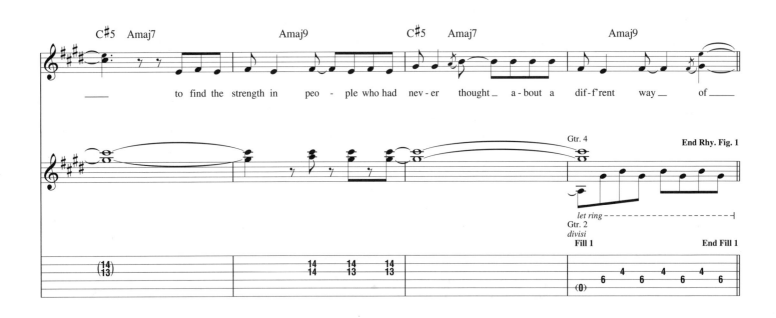

℅ Pre-Chorus

Half-time feel

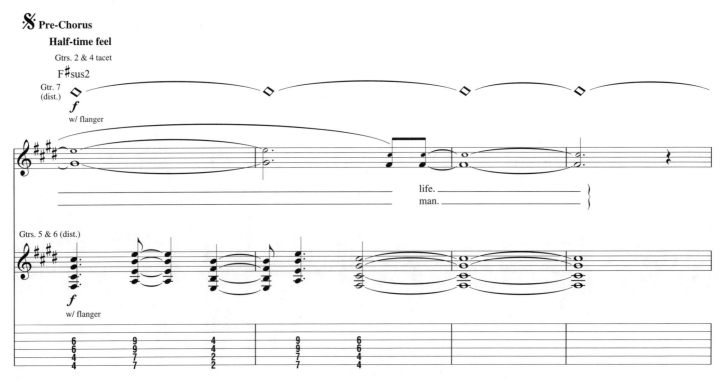

End half-time feel

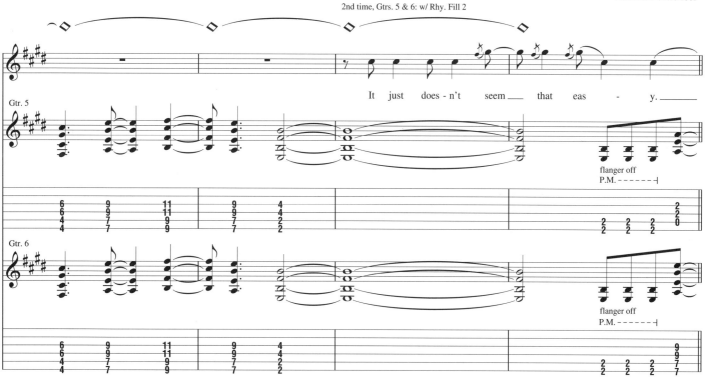

It just does-n't seem___ that eas - y.___

Chorus

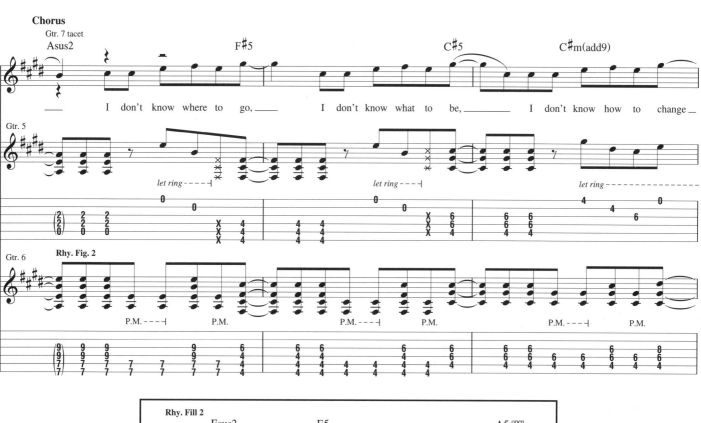

I don't know where to go,___ I don't know what to be,_____ I don't know how to change___

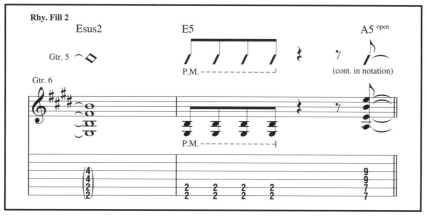

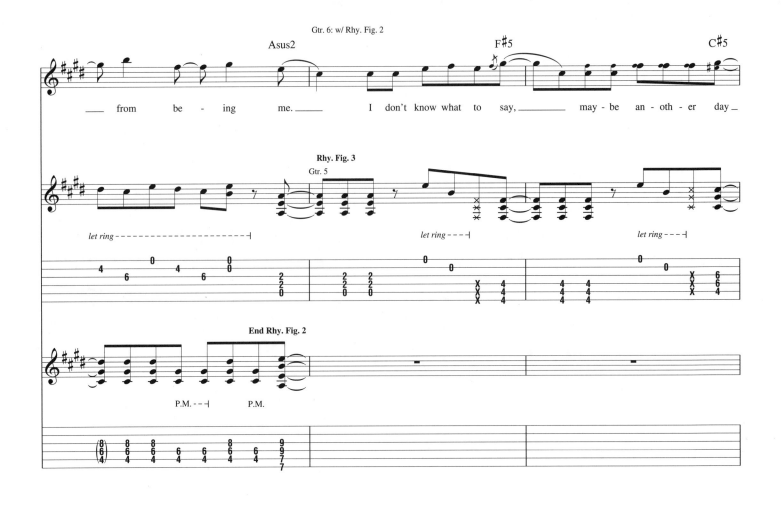

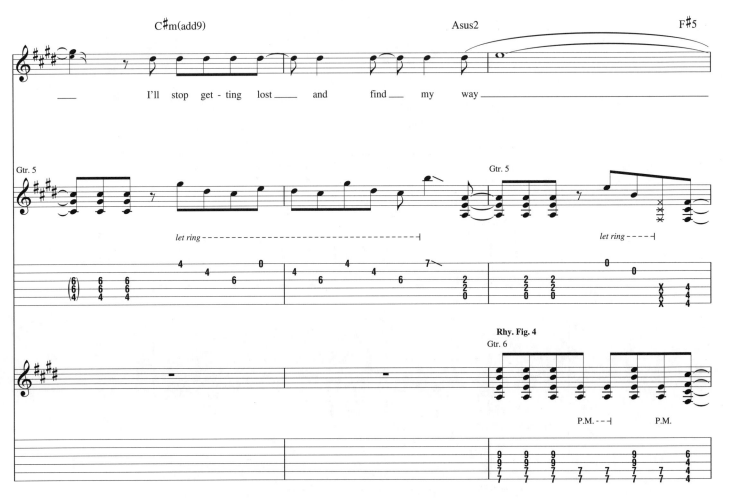

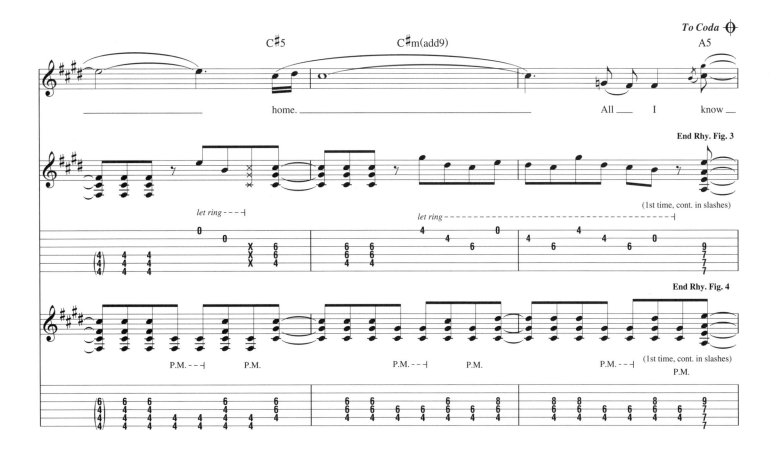

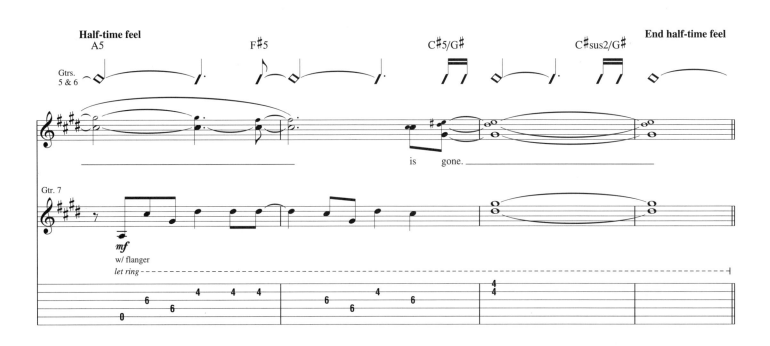

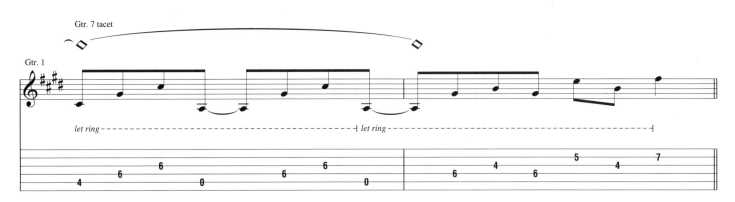

Verse

Gtr. 1: w/ Riff A (1 7/8 times)
Gtr. 4: w/ Rhy. Fig. 1
Gtrs. 5 & 6 tacet

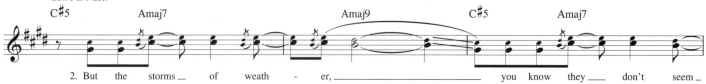

2. But the storms __ of weath - er, _____ you know they __ don't seem __

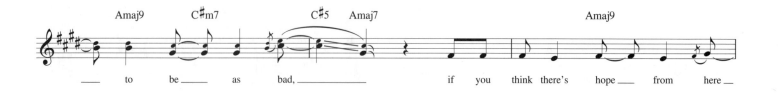

__ to be __ as bad, _____ if you think there's hope __ from here __

Gtr. 3: w/ Rhy. Fill 1

__ and there's __ a life __ you should __ now have. I don't __ have an -

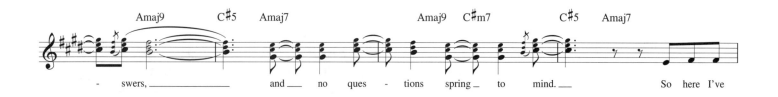

- swers, _____ and __ no ques - tions spring __ to mind. __ So here I've

D.S. al Coda

Gtr. 1: w/ Fill 1

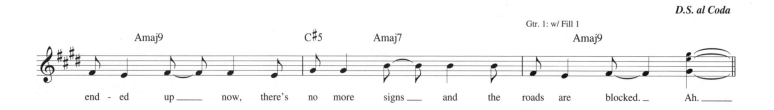

end - ed up __ now, there's no more signs __ and the roads are blocked. _ Ah. _____

Coda

Half-time feel

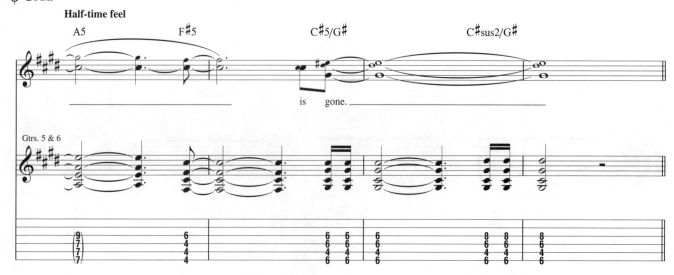

is gone.

Gtrs. 5 & 6

56

Bridge

Gtrs. 5 & 6 tacet

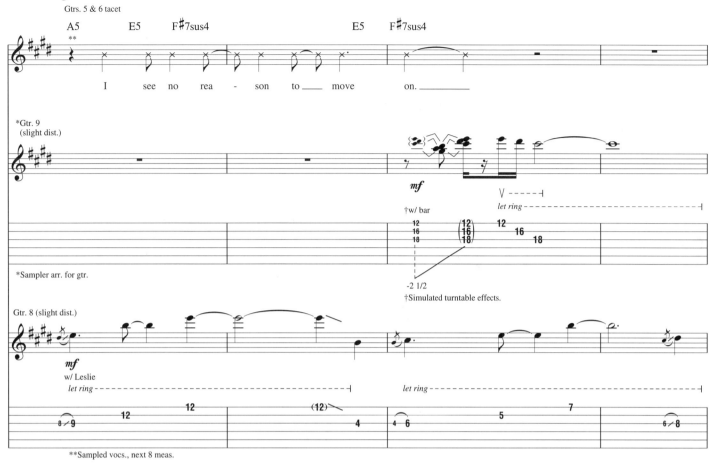

I see no rea - son to __ move on. __

*Gtr. 9
(slight dist.)

mf

†w/ bar

let ring

-2 1/2

†Simulated turntable effects.

*Sampler arr. for gtr.

Gtr. 8 (slight dist.)

mf

w/ Leslie

let ring

**Sampled vocs., next 8 meas.

End half-time feel

I see no rea - son to __ move o - o - o - on. __

let ring

let ring

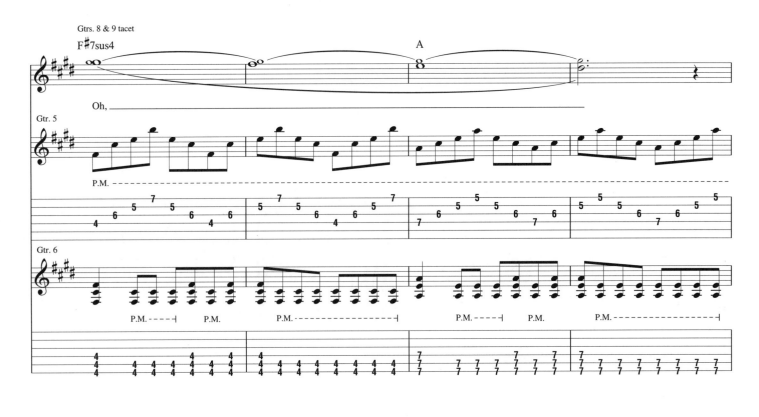

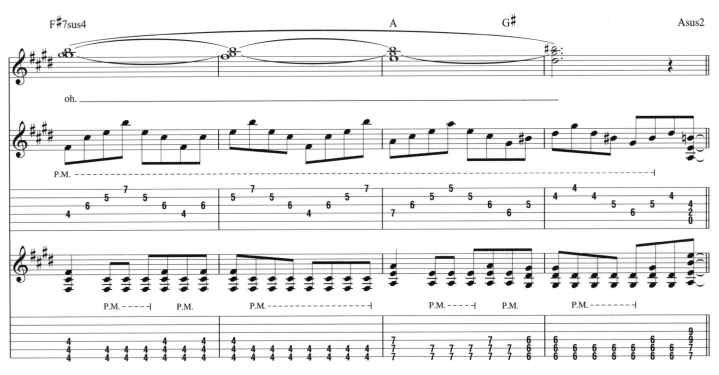

Chorus

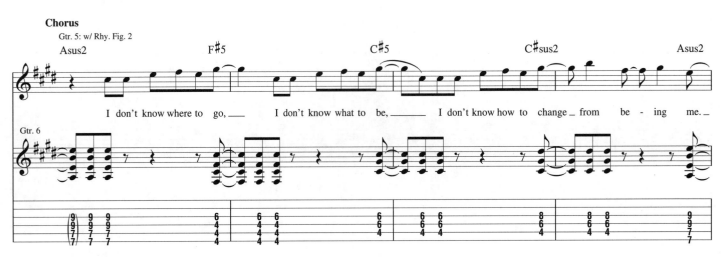

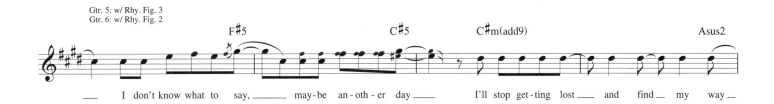

I don't know what to say,___ may-be an-oth-er day ___ I'll stop get-ting lost ___ and find ___ my way ___

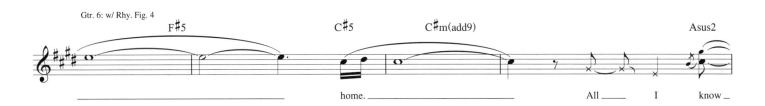

home. ___ All ___ I know ___

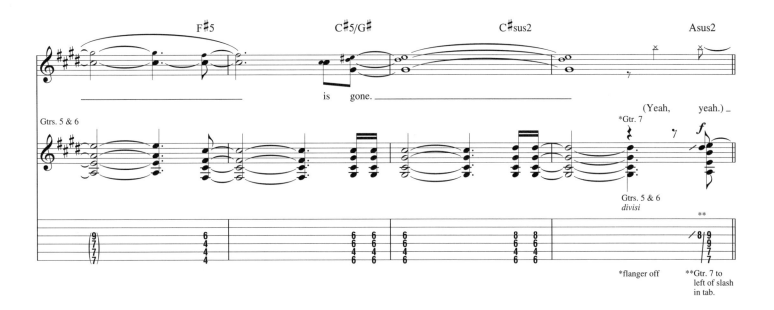

is gone. ___

(Yeah, yeah.) ___

*flanger off   **Gtr. 7 to left of slash in tab.

Guitar Solo

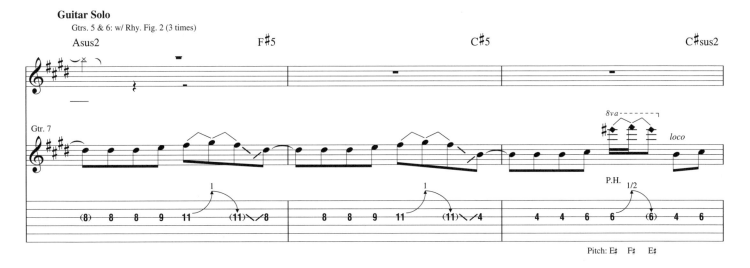

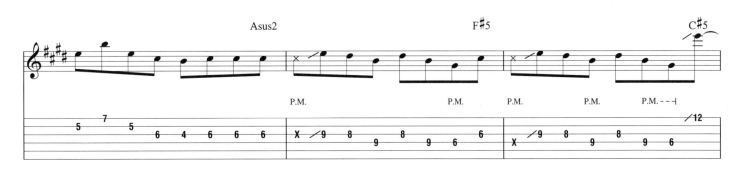

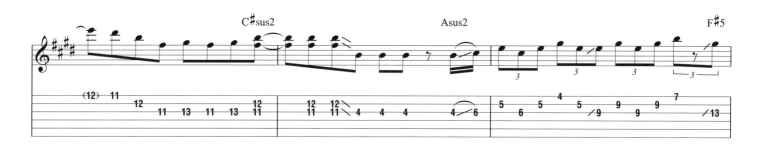

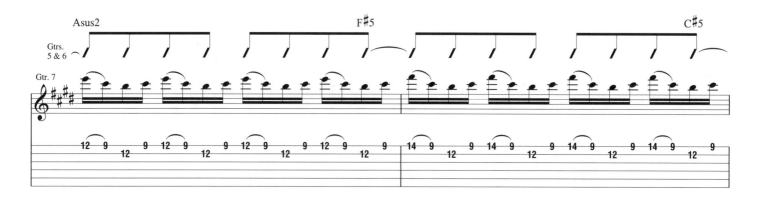

Outro

Segue to "Hello Again"

Gtrs. 5, 6 & 7 tacet

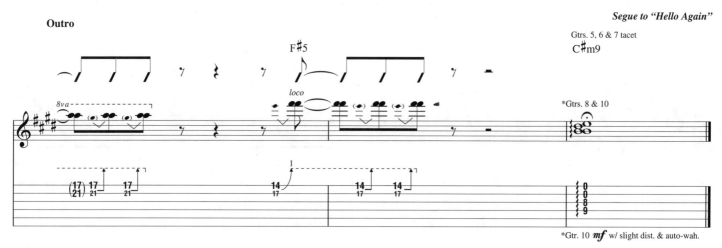

*Gtr. 10 **mf** w/ slight dist. & auto-wah.

Hello Again

Words and Music by Michael Lewis, Ian Watkins, Richard Oliver, Lee Gaze, Stuart Richardson and Michael Chiplin

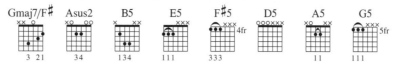

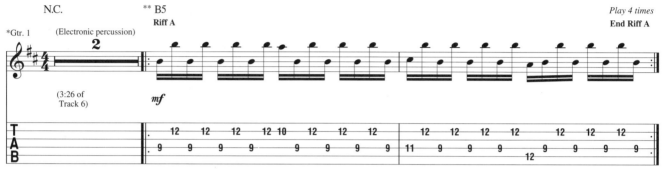

Drop D tuning:
(low to high) D-A-D-G-B-E

Intro

Moderately slow ♩ = 80

***Track 7 starts here.

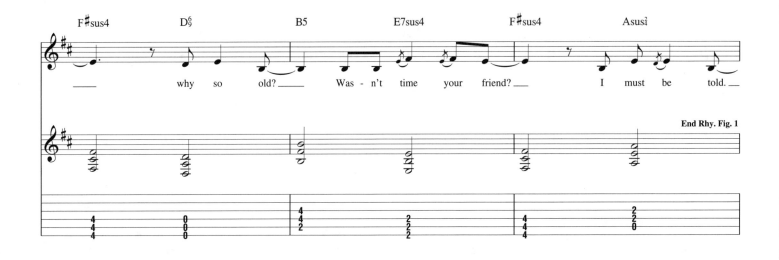

why so old? _____ Was - n't time your friend? _____ I must be told. _____

End Rhy. Fig. 1

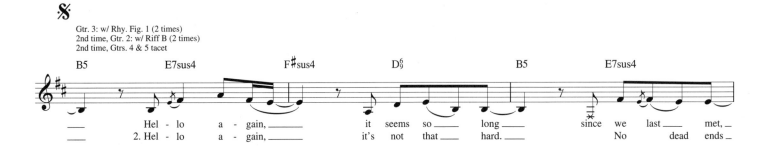

Gtr. 3: w/ Rhy. Fig. 1 (2 times)
2nd time, Gtr. 2: w/ Riff B (2 times)
2nd time, Gtrs. 4 & 5 tacet

_____ Hel - lo a - gain, _____ it seems so _____ long _____ since we last _____ met, _____
2. Hel - lo a - gain, _____ it's not that _____ hard. _____ No dead ends _____

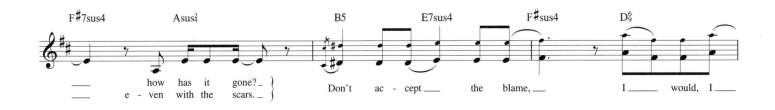

_____ how has it gone? _____ Don't ac - cept _____ the blame, _____ I _____ would, I _____
_____ e - ven with the scars. _____

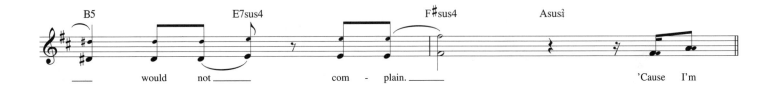

_____ would not _____ com - plain. _____ 'Cause I'm

Pre-Chorus
1st time, Gtr. 2: w/ Riff B (1 1/2 times)
2nd time, Gtr. 2: w/ Riff B

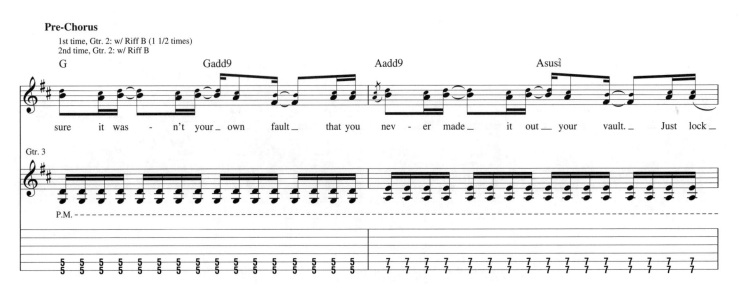

sure it was - n't your _____ own fault _____ that you nev - er made _____ it out _____ your vault. _____ Just lock

Gtr. 3

P.M. -

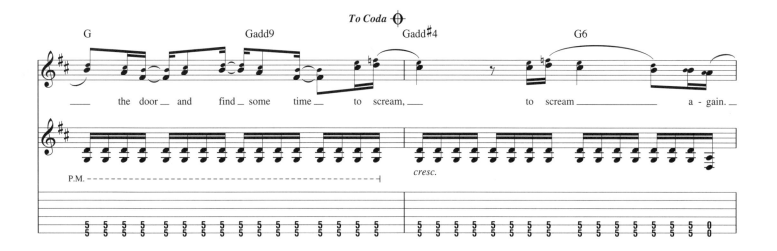

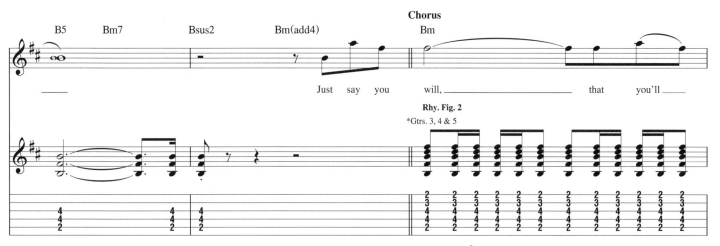

*Gtr. 4 (elec.) *mf* w/ dist. Gtr. 5 (acous.) *mp*. Composite arrangement

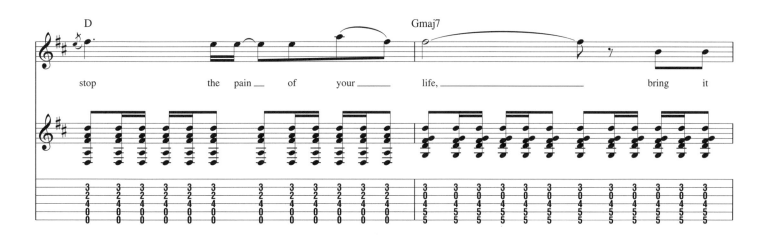

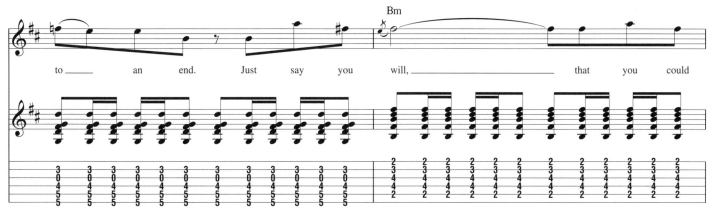

make _____ a-mends. Just say hel - lo, _____ say hel - lo _____ a - gain.

Coda

Chorus
Gtrs. 3, 4 & 5: w/ Rhy. Fig. 2

Just say you will, _____ that you'll _____ stop the pain _ of your _____

life, _____ bring it to _____ an end. Just say you will, _____ that you could

make _____ a-mends. _____ Just say hel - lo, _____ say hel - lo _____ a - gain.

Interlude

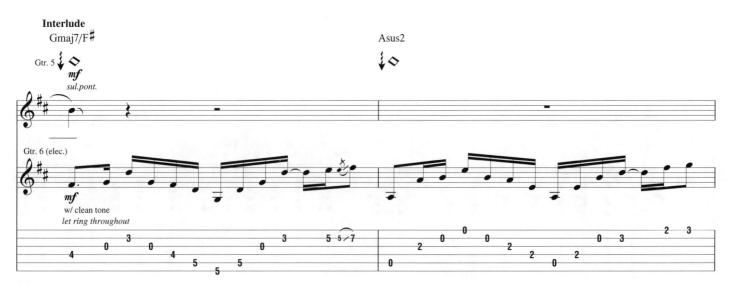

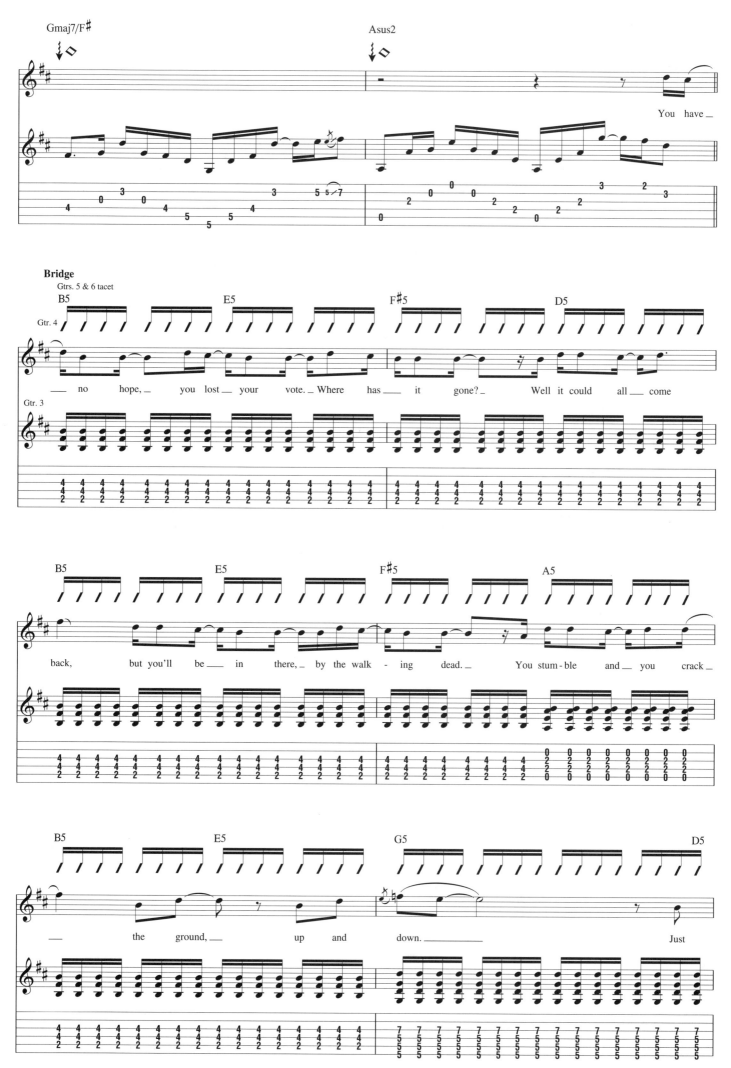

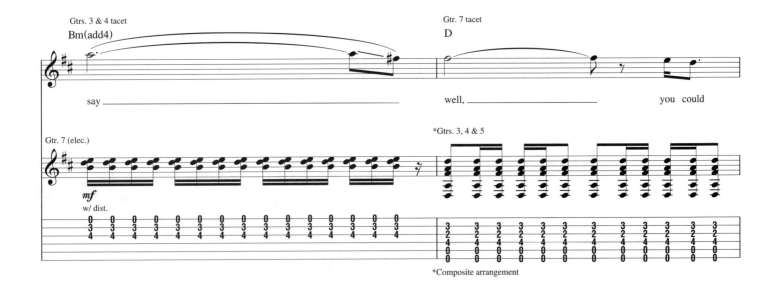

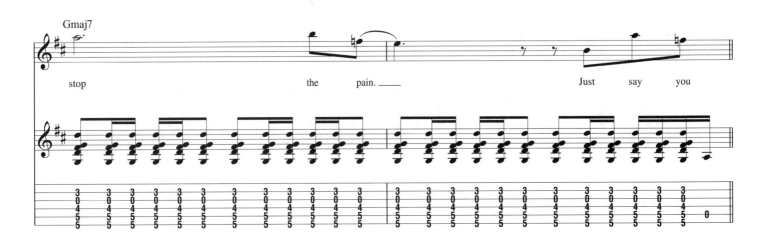

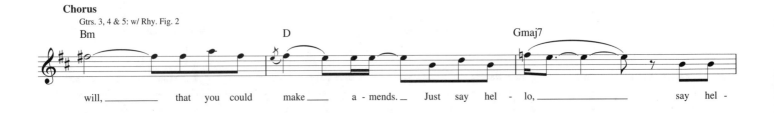

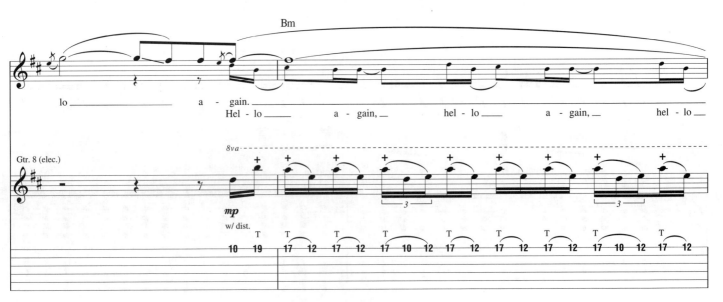

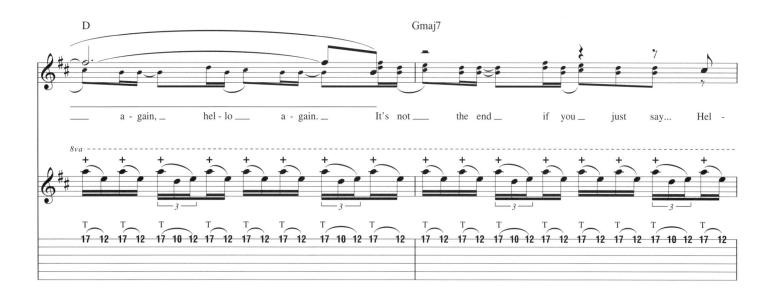

a - gain, ___ hel - lo ___ a - gain. ___ It's not ___ the end ___ if you ___ just say... Hel -

Outro
Gtr. 2: w/ Riff B (2 times)
Gtr. 8 tacet

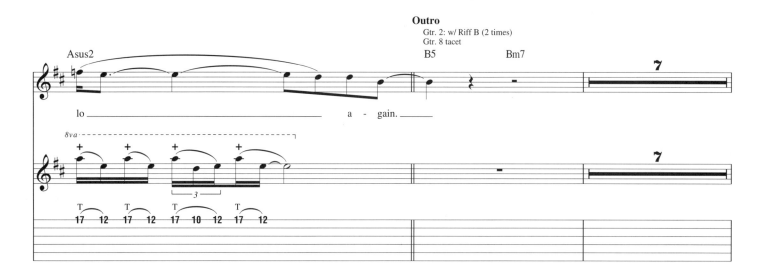

lo ___ a - gain. ___

Faster ♩ = 91
Gtr. 2 tacet

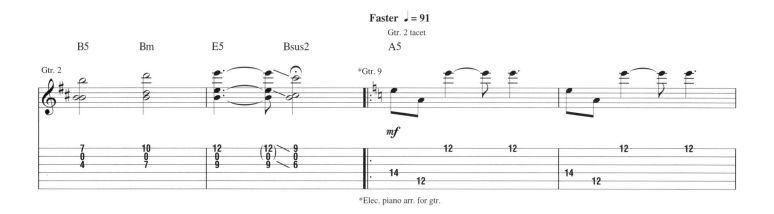

*Elec. piano arr. for gtr.

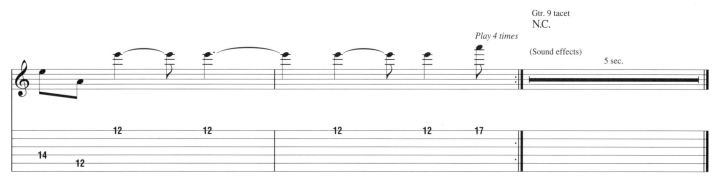

Goodbye Tonight

Words and Music by Michael Lewis, Ian Watkins, Richard Oliver, Lee Gaze, Stuart Richardson and Michael Chiplin

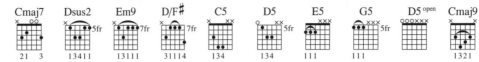

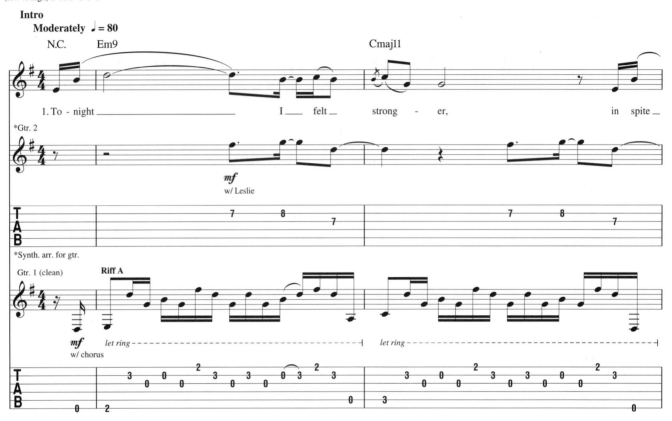

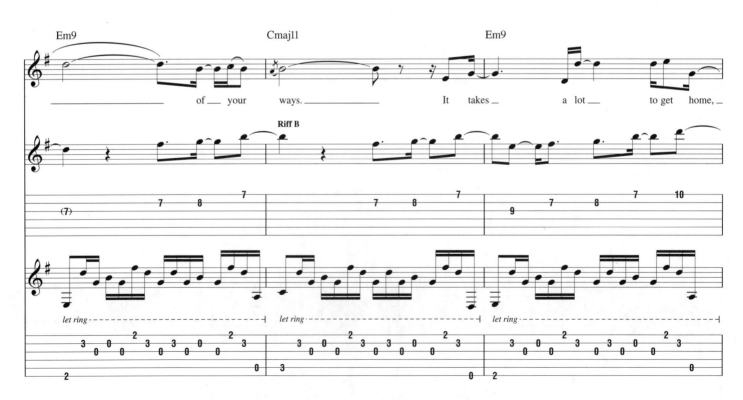

but it's __ o - kay __ when the light __ is al - ways __ on.

End Riff B

End Riff A

let ring - - - - - - - - - - - - - - - - - - *let ring* - - - - - - - - - - - - - - - - *let ring* - - - - - - - - - - - - - - - - - - -

(cont. in slashes)

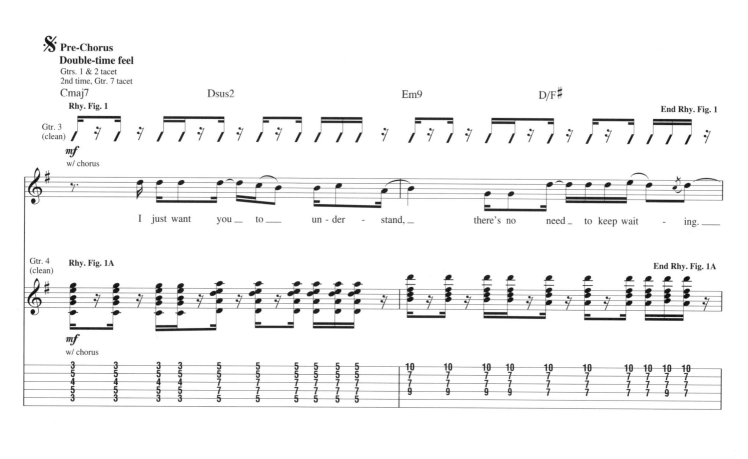

𝄋 **Pre-Chorus**
Double-time feel
Gtrs. 1 & 2 tacet
2nd time, Gtr. 7 tacet

Rhy. Fig. 1

Gtr. 3
(clean)

mf
w/ chorus

End Rhy. Fig. 1

I just want you __ to __ un - der - stand, __ there's no need __ to keep wait - ing. __

Gtr. 4
(clean)

Rhy. Fig. 1A

End Rhy. Fig. 1A

mf
w/ chorus

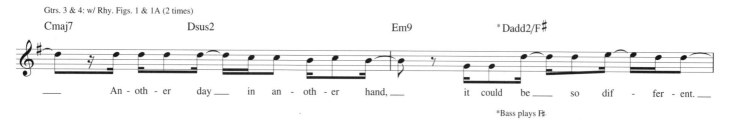

Gtrs. 3 & 4: w/ Rhy. Figs. 1 & 1A (2 times)

__ An - oth - er day __ in an - oth - er hand, __ it could be __ so dif - fer - ent. __

*Bass plays F♯.

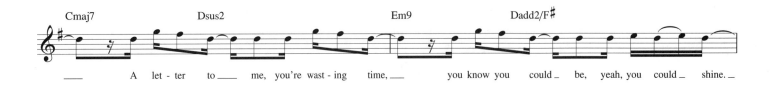

A let-ter to ___ me, you're wast-ing time, ___ you know you could ___ be, yeah, you could ___ shine. ___

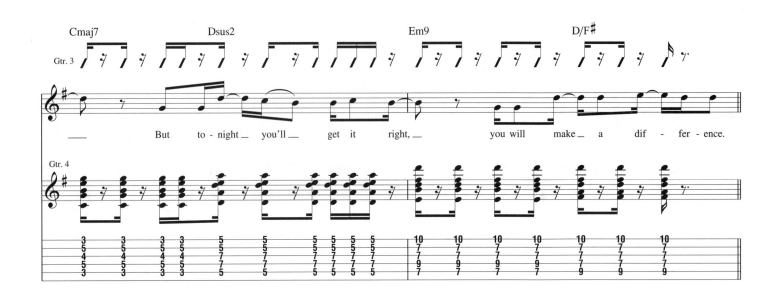

___ But to-night ___ you'll ___ get it right, ___ you will make a dif-fer-ence.

Chorus

A, to-night, __ to-night, __ to-night, __ feel __ strong-

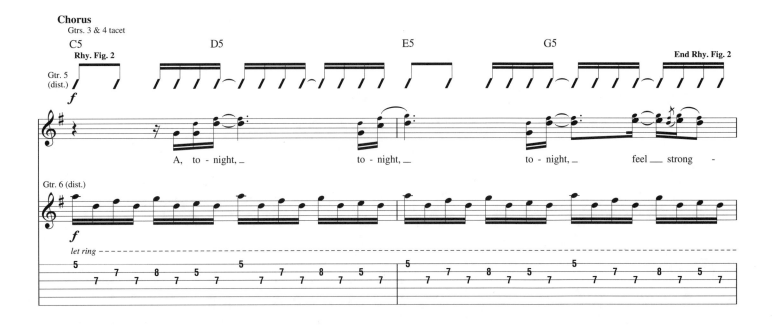

er. Good-bye, __ good-bye, _____ good-bye, _____ If I ___ could

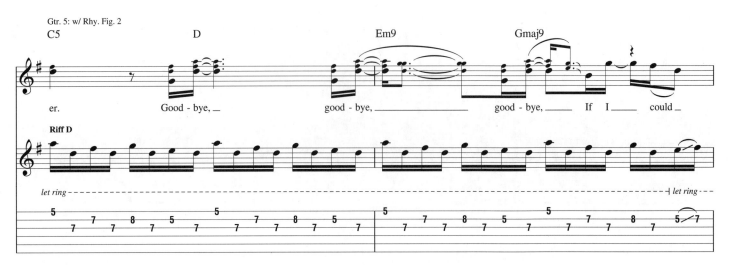

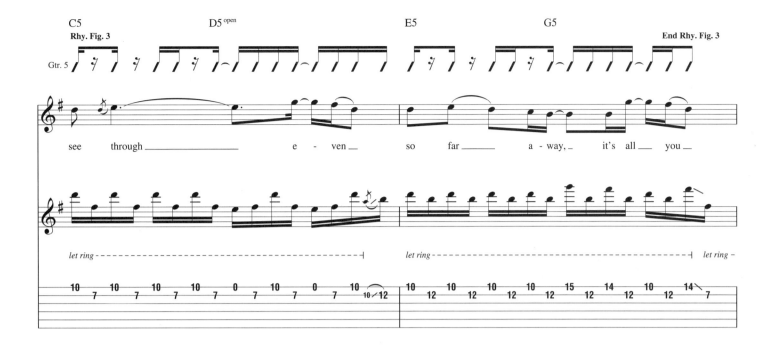

see through _____ e - ven __ so far _____ a - way, __ it's all __ you __

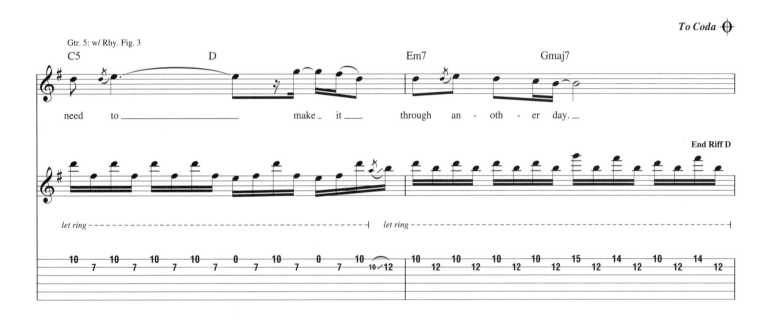

need to _____ make __ it __ through an - oth - er day. __

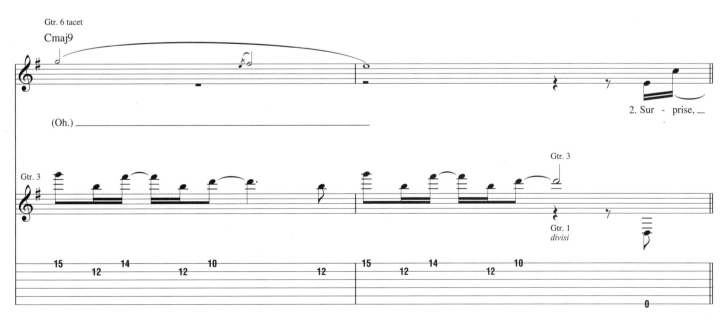

(Oh.) _____

2. Sur - prise, __

Verse

Gtr. 1: w/ Riff A
Gtr. 3 tacet

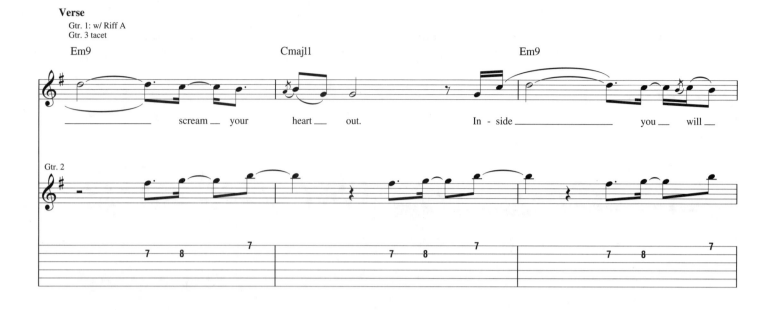

Gtr. 2: w/ Riff B

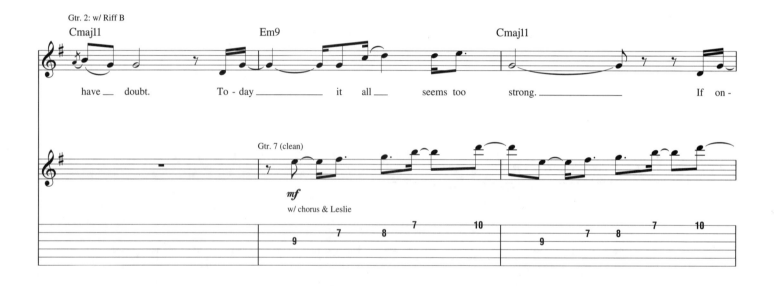

D.S. al Coda

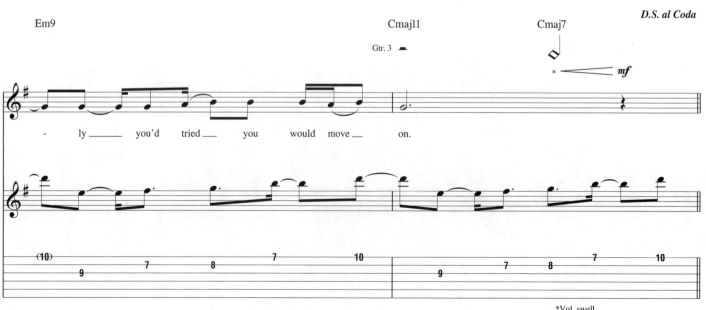

*Vol. swell

Coda

Interlude
Cmaj9

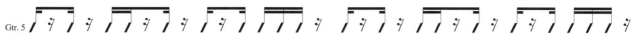

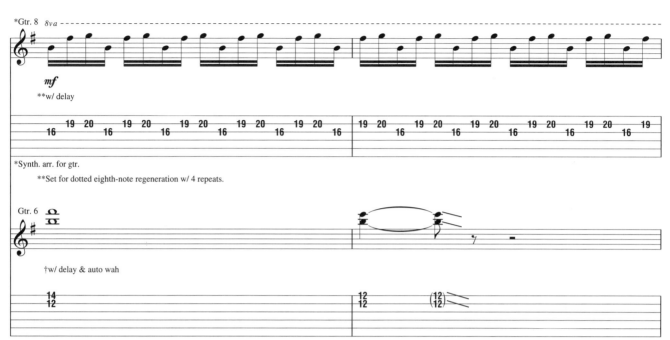

*Synth. arr. for gtr.

**Set for dotted eighth-note regeneration w/ 4 repeats.

†w/ delay & auto wah

†Set for eighth-note regeneration w/ infinite repeats.

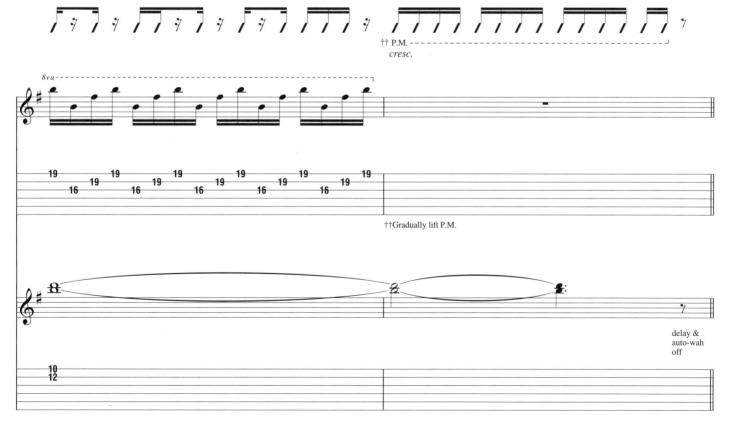

†† P.M.

cresc.

††Gradually lift P.M.

delay &
auto-wah

Chorus

Gtr. 8 tacet

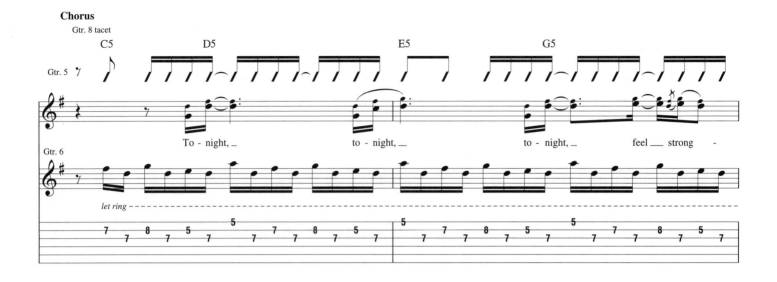

Gtr. 5: w/ Rhy. Fig. 2 (3 times)

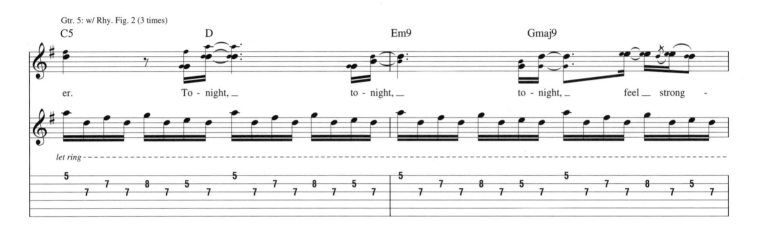

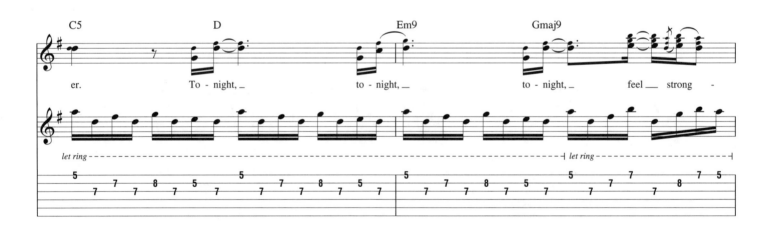

Gtr. 6: w/ Riff D   Gtr. 5: w/ Rhy. Fig. 3 (1 1/2 times)

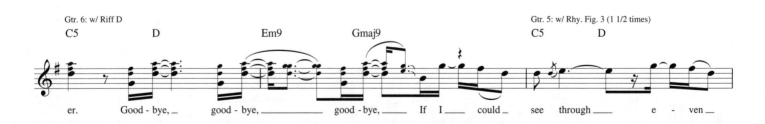

74

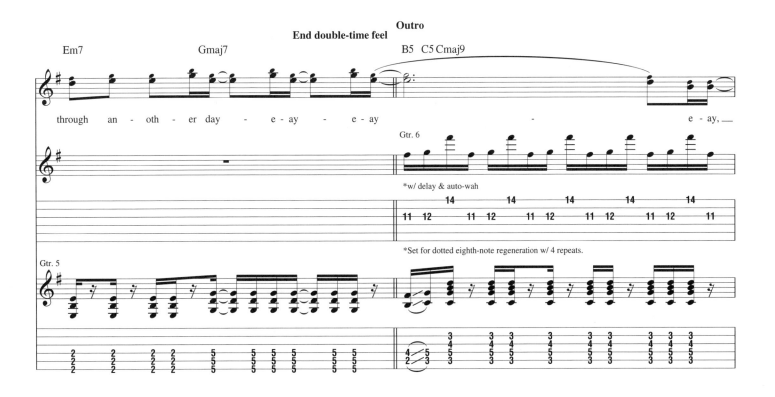

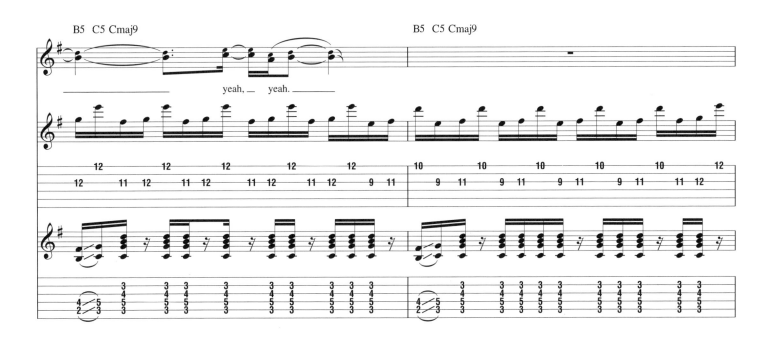

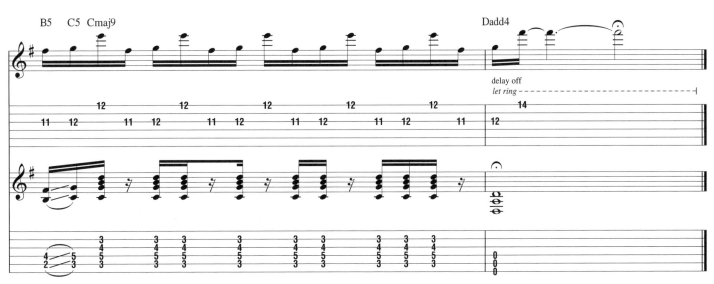

Start Something

Words and Music by Michael Lewis, Ian Watkins, Richard Oliver, Lee Gaze, Stuart Richardson and Michael Chiplin

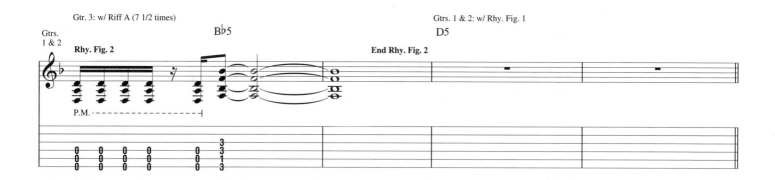

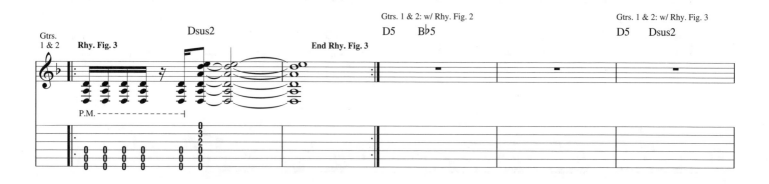

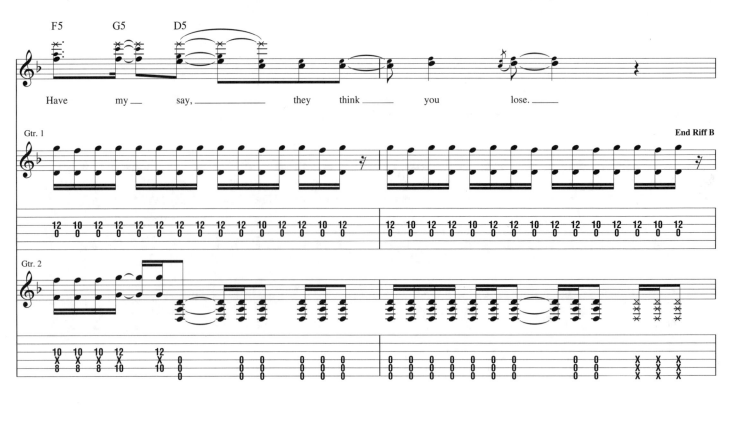

Have my __ say, ____ they think ____ you __ lose. __

Gtr. 1

End Riff B

Gtr. 2

Gtr. 1: w/ Riff B
Gtr. 2: w/ Rhy. Fig. 4 (2 times)

For all __ this, __ you mean __ so much to me. For all __ this, __ you make __ a move. ____

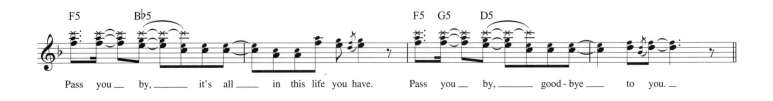

Pass you __ by, ____ it's all __ in this life you have. Pass you __ by, ____ good - bye ___ to you. __

Interlude

2nd time, Gtr. 3 tacet   Gtr. 2 tacet   Gtrs. 1 & 2: w/ Riff C

D5

Rhy. Fill 1   **End Rhy. Fill 1**

Gtr. 2

(Yeah.) ____   One, two, three, four. Ow.

Gtr. 1   **Riff C**   **End Riff C**

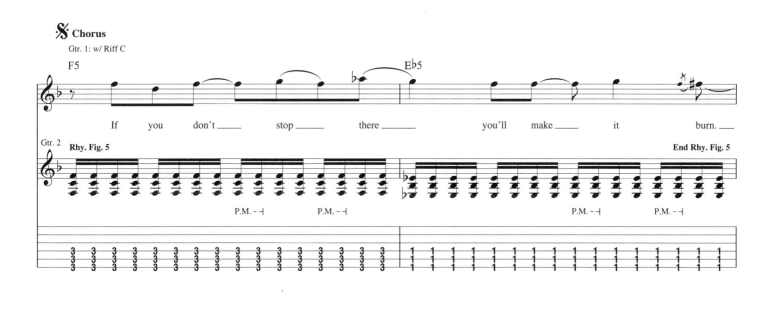

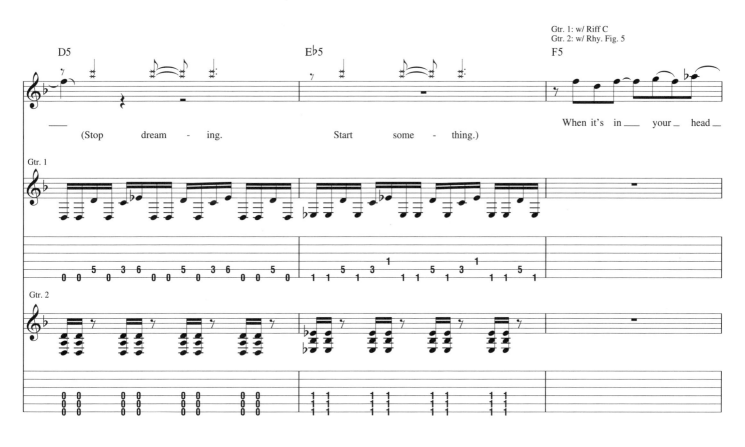

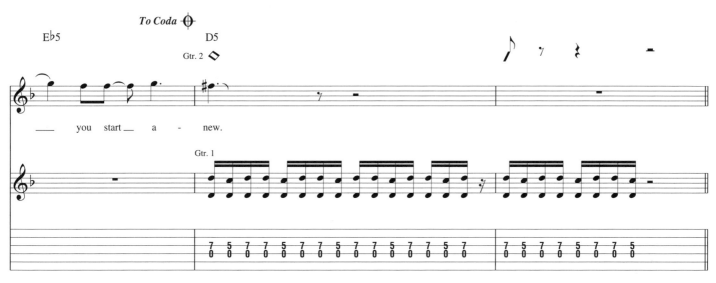

Verse

Gtr. 1: w/ Riff B (2 times)
Gtr. 2: w/ Rhy. Fig. 4 (4 times)

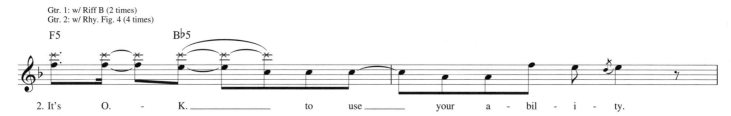

2. It's O. - K. _____ to use _____ your a - bil - i - ty.

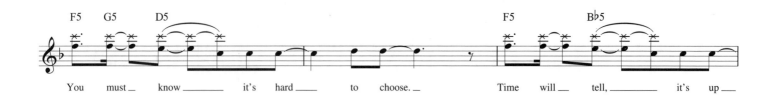

You must _ know _____ it's hard __ to choose. _ Time will _ tell, _____ it's up __

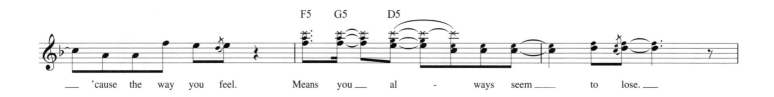

__ 'cause the way you feel. Means you _ al - ways seem __ to lose. __

Seize the _ day, _____ the one _____ that you left be - hind.

Gtr. 3

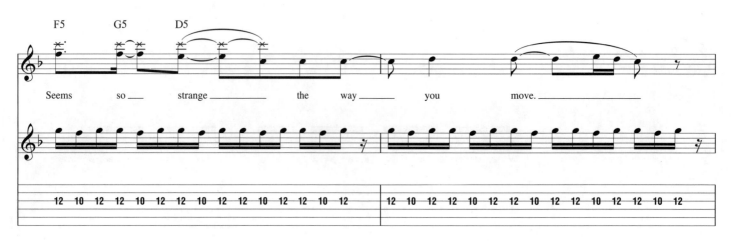

Seems so _ strange _____ the way ____ you move. _____

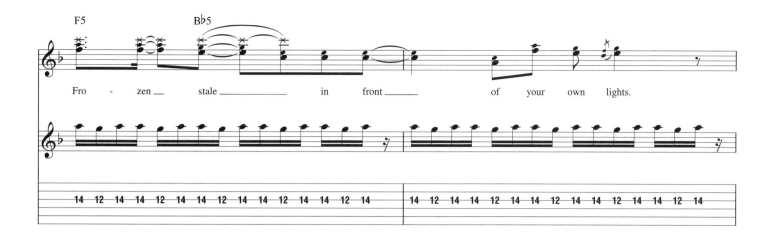

Fro - zen ___ stale ___ in front ___ of your own lights.

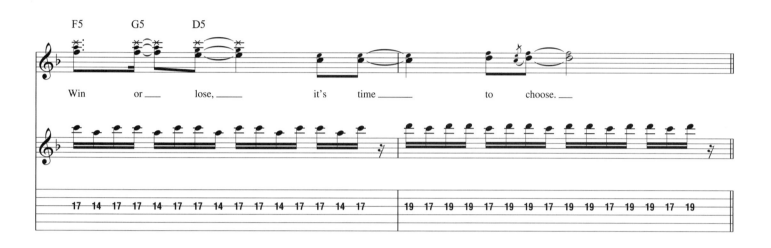

Win or ___ lose, ___ it's time ___ to choose. ___

D. S. al Coda

Interlude
Gtr. 1: w/ Riff C (2 times)
Gtr. 2: w/ Rhy. Fill 1
Gtr. 3 tacet

Gtr. 2: w/ Riff C

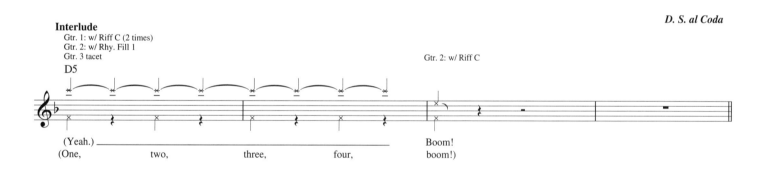

(Yeah.) ___
(One, two, three, four, Boom! boom!)

⊕ **Coda**
Outro
Half-time feel

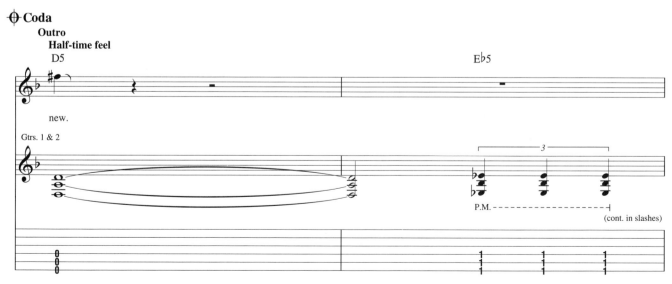

new.

Gtrs. 1 & 2

81

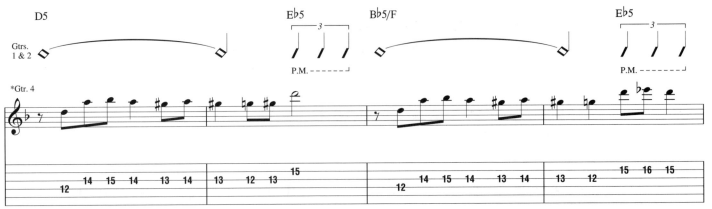

*Piano arr. for gtr.

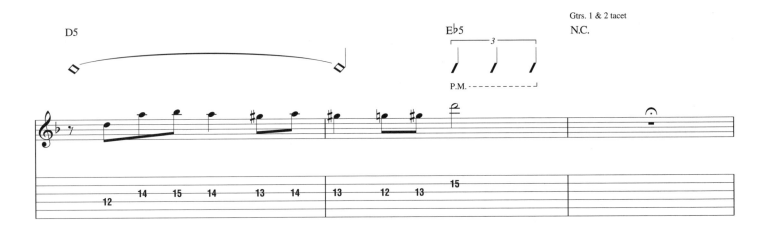

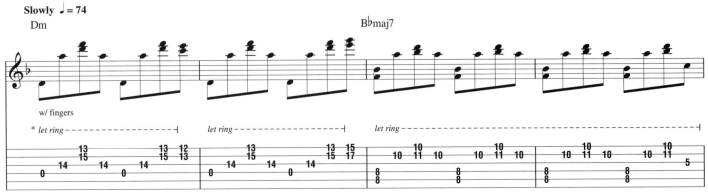

*Let 4th string ring throughout (next 2 meas.)

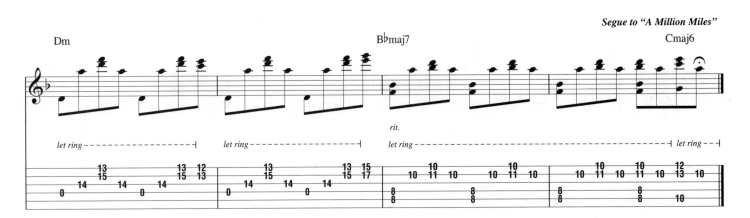

A Million Miles

Words and Music by Michael Lewis, Ian Watkins, Richard Oliver, Lee Gaze, Stuart Richardson and Michael Chiplin

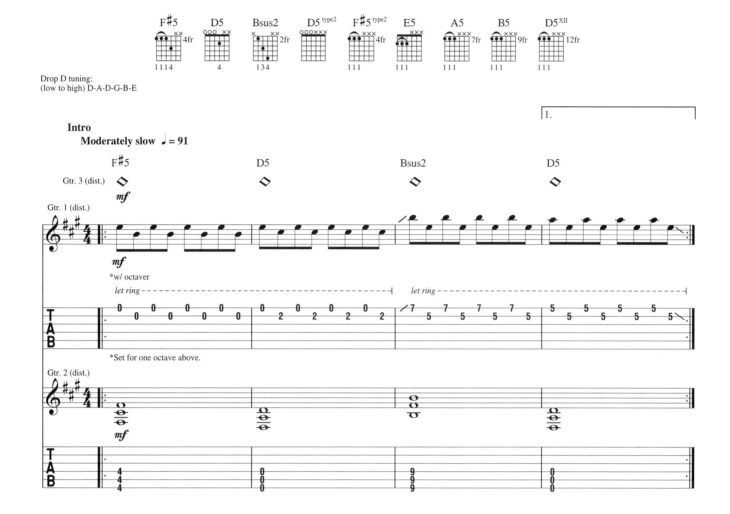

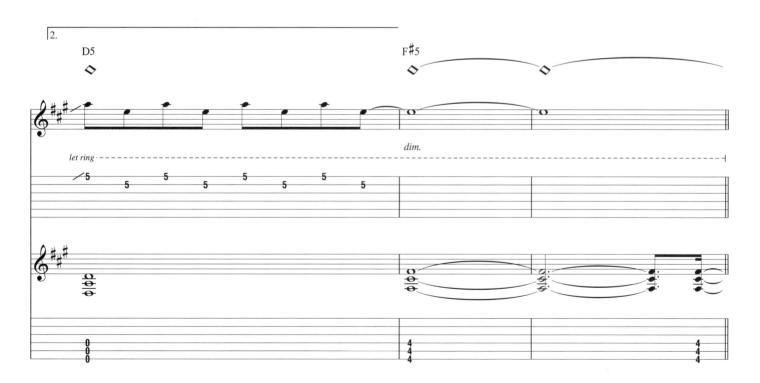

Verse

1. I hear you scream-ing but I know that you don't mean it, and it's...

All gone wrong now.
Screamed: (Got-ta, got-ta, got-ta take con-trol. Con-trol, got-ta, got-ta, got-ta take con-trol.)

*Applies to Bkgd. Voc. only.

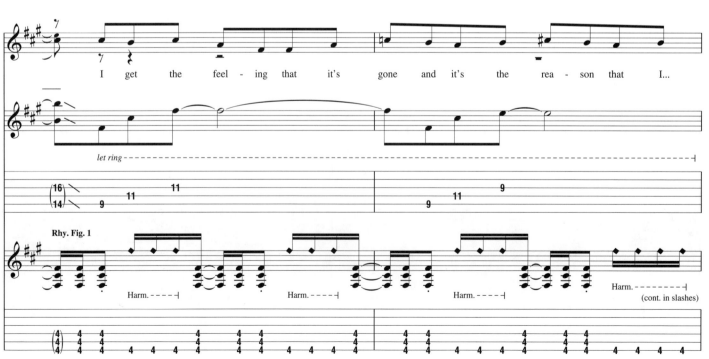

I get the feel-ing that it's gone and it's the rea-son that I...

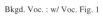

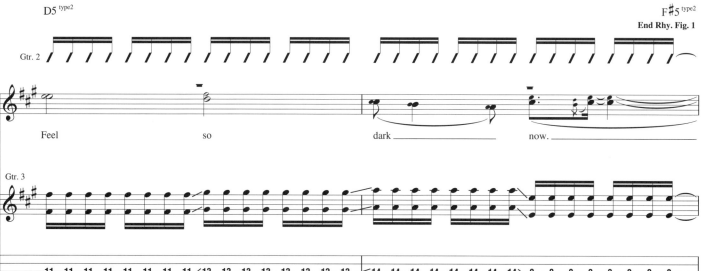

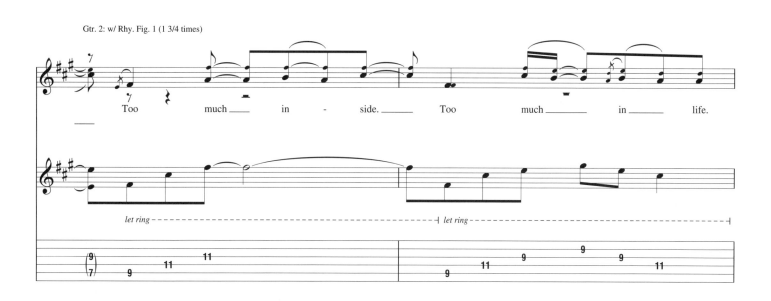

*Applies to Bkgd. Voc. only.

I know you're leav-ing though I think that my time's fleet-ing, but yet... You don't
Spoken: (Five, four,

As before.

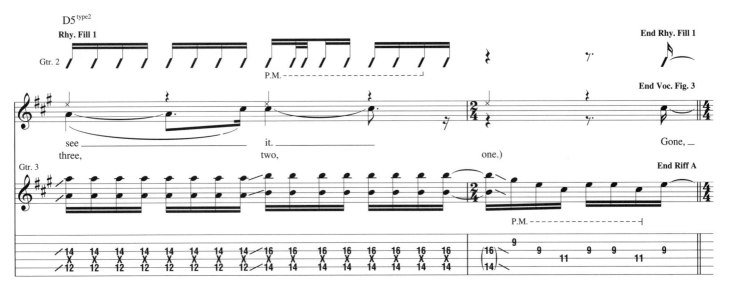

see it.
three, two, one.)
Gone,

once you've shown how to move on though I still find time to hide.

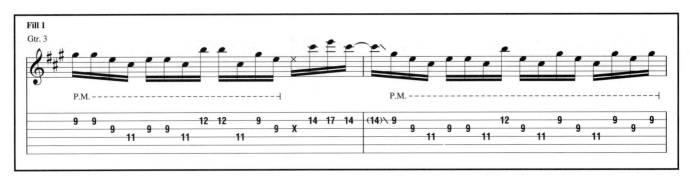

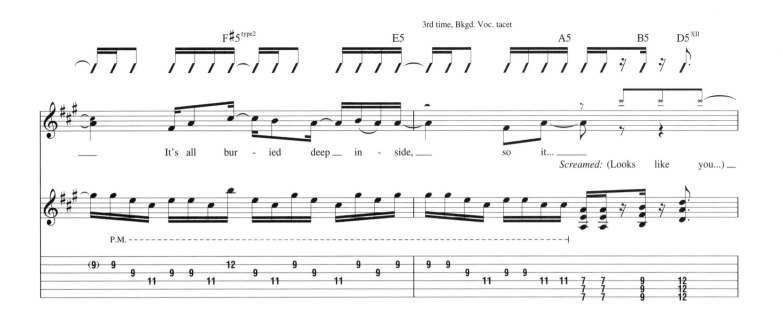

It's all bur-ied deep _ in - side, _ so it... _ *Screamed:* (Looks like you...) _

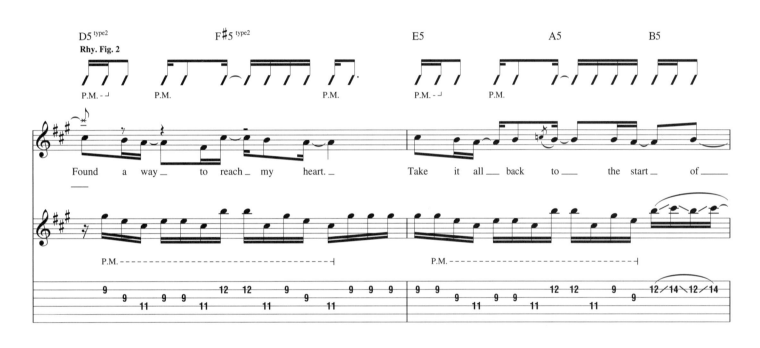

Found a way _ to reach _ my heart. _ Take it all _ back to _ the start _ of _

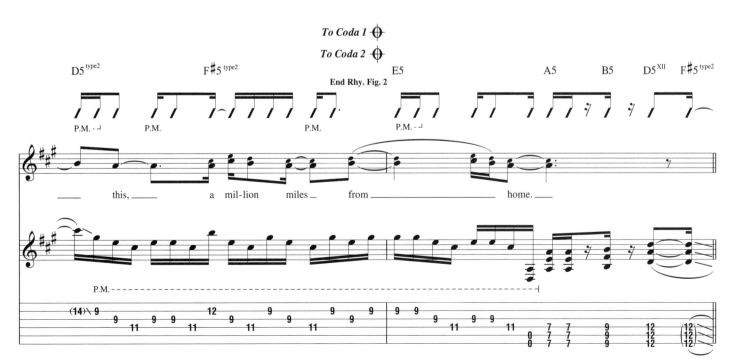

this, _ a mil-lion miles _ from _ home. _

Verse

Gtr. 2: w/ Rhy. Fig. 1 (3 3/4 times)

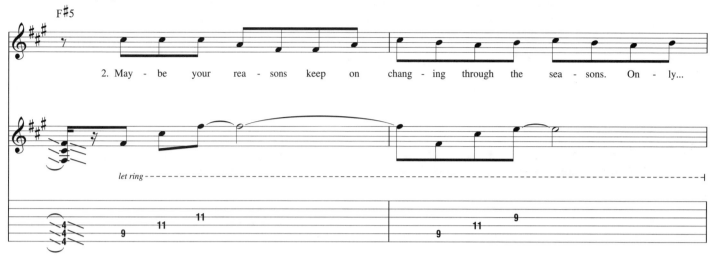

2. May - be your rea - sons keep on chang - ing through the sea - sons. On - ly...

let ring

Bkgd. Voc.: w/ Voc. Fig. 1
Gtr. 3: w/ Riff A

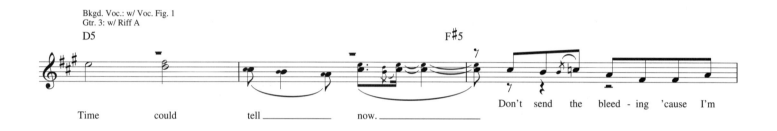

Time could tell _____ now. _____ Don't send the bleed - ing 'cause I'm

Bkgd. Voc.: w/ Voc. Fig. 1

sure it has a mean - ing. Still you... Feel so dark _____ now.

Bkgd. Voc.: w/ Voc. Fig. 2

Too much __ in - side. ___ Too much _____ in ___ life. ___ De - fine

your point of view. _____ Are you still leav - ing? May - be you should start be - liev - ing, but still...

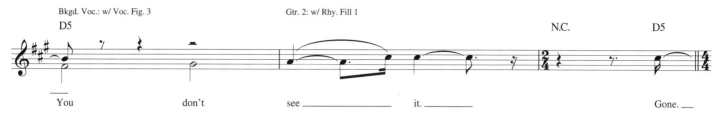

$\bigoplus$ **Coda 1**

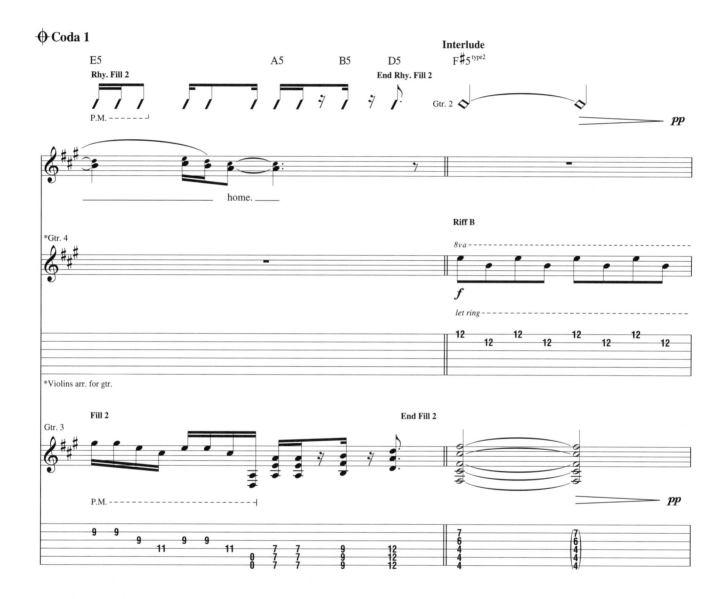

Interlude

Riff B

Fill 2

End Fill 2

*Violins arr. for gtr.

Gtr. 3

Gtrs. 2 & 3 tacet

Gtr. 4: w/ Riff B

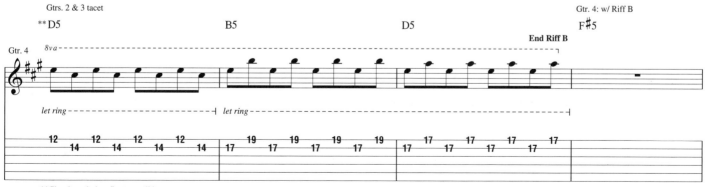

**D5

B5

D5

F#5

End Riff B

Gtr. 4

**Chord symbols reflect overall harmony.

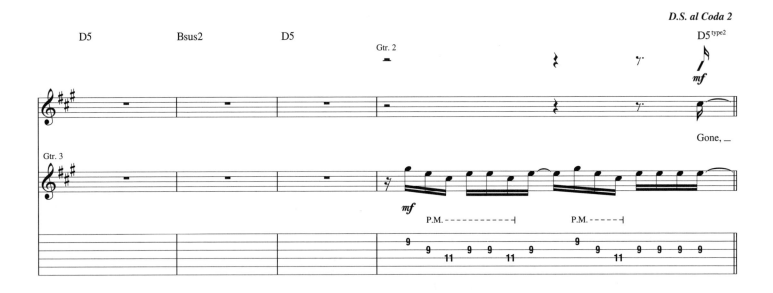

⊕ Coda 2

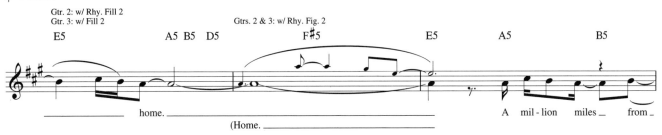

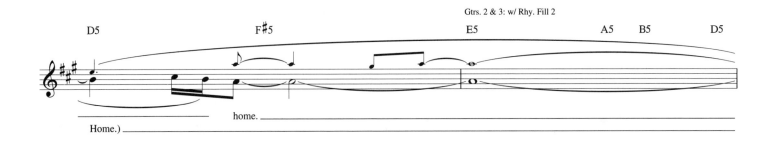

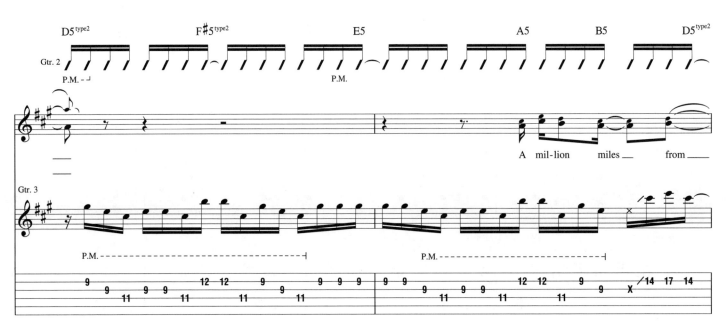

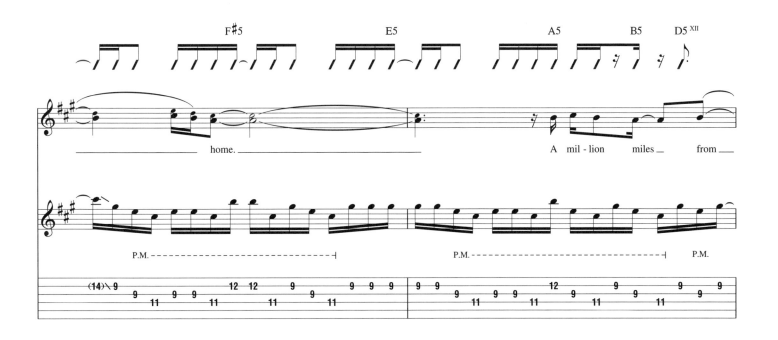

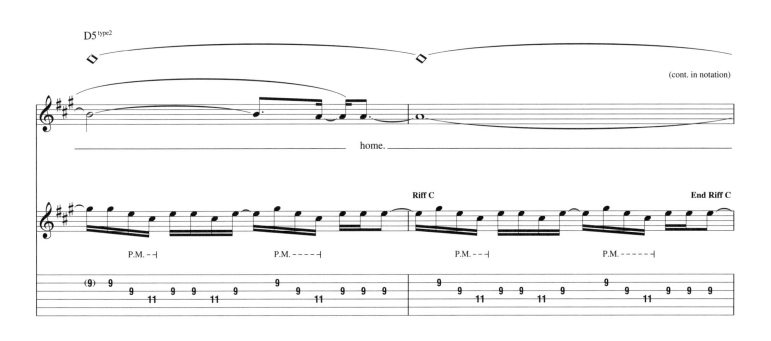

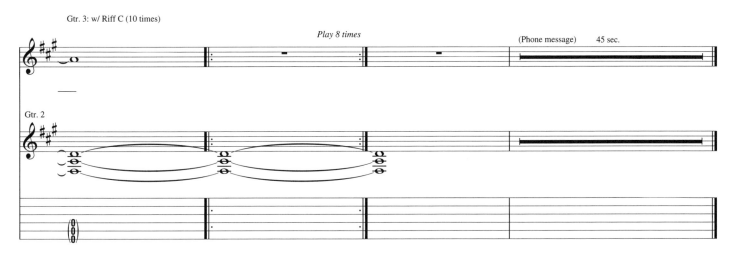

Last Summer

Words and Music by Michael Lewis, Ian Watkins, Richard Oliver, Lee Gaze, Stuart Richardson and Michael Chiplin

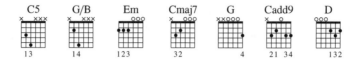

Gtrs. 1-4: Drop D tuning:
(low to high) D-A-D-G-B-E
Gtr. 5: Drop B tuning:
(low to high) B♭-A-D-G-B-E

Intro
Moderately fast ♩ = 140

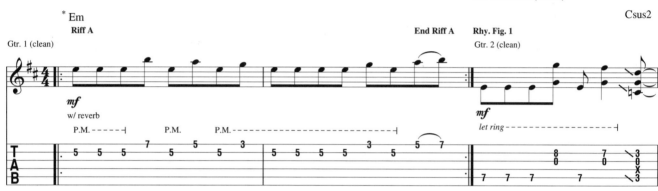

*Chord symbols reflect implied harmony.

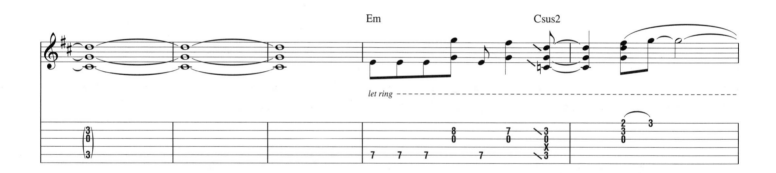

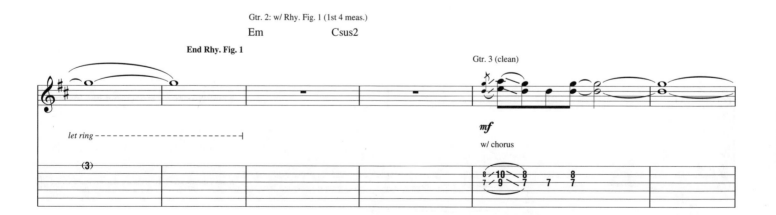

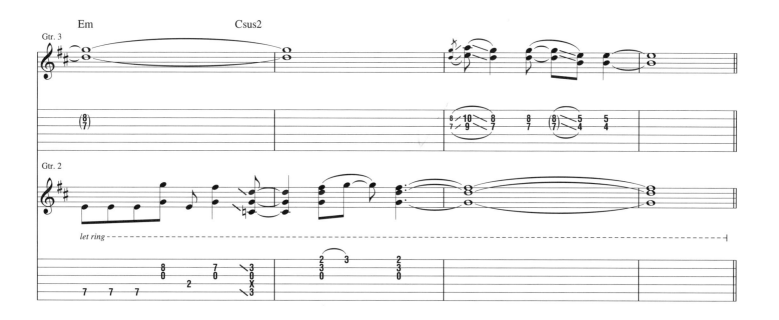

Verse

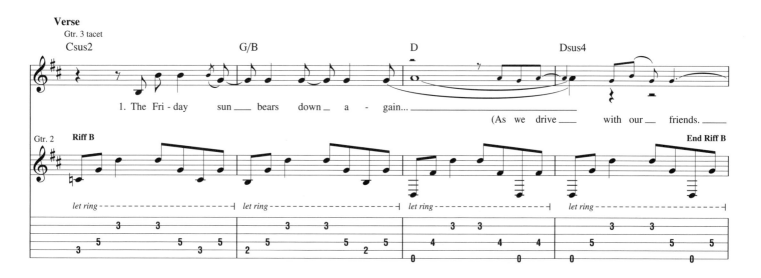

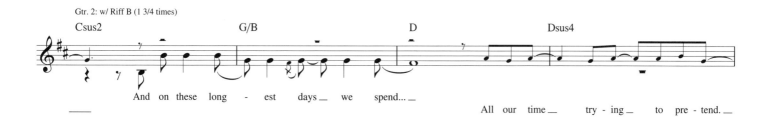

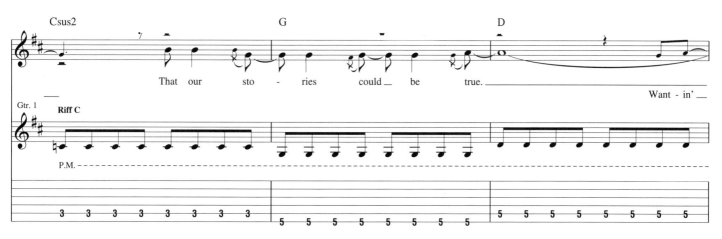

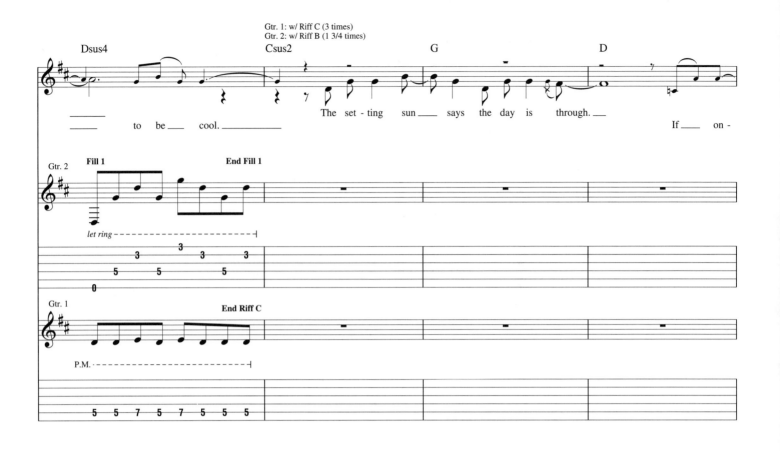

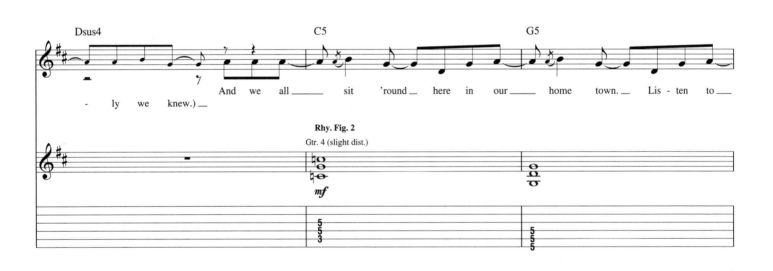

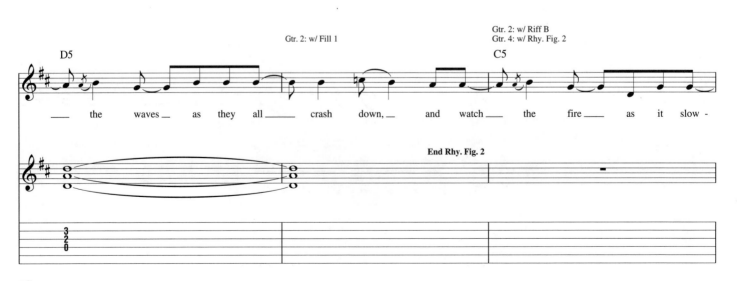

-ly burns ___ a - way. ___   Glow - ing

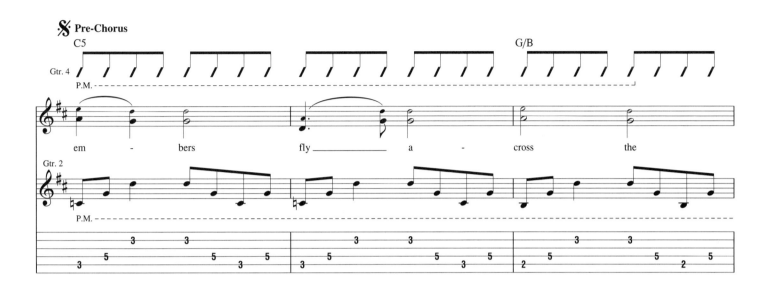

S. Pre-Chorus

em - bers ___ fly ___ a - cross ___ the

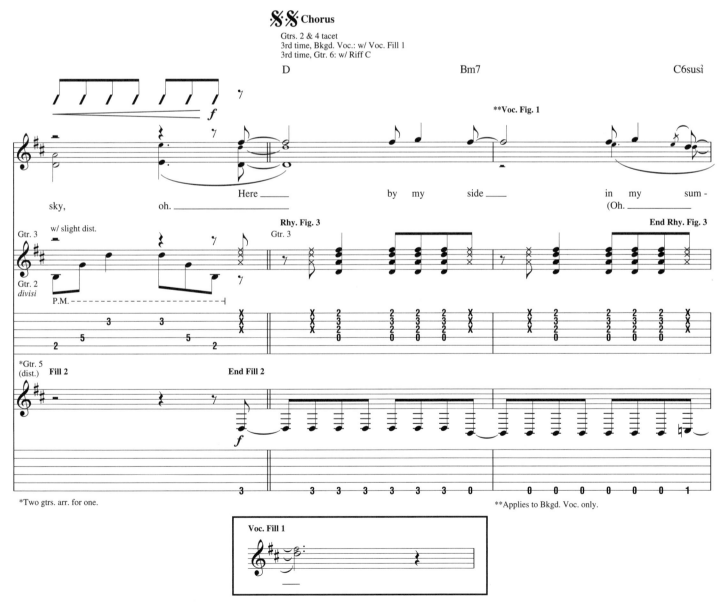

Gtrs. 2 & 4 tacet
3rd time, Bkgd. Voc.: w/ Voc. Fill 1
3rd time, Gtr. 6: w/ Riff C

sky,   oh. ___   Here ___ by my side ___ in my sum-
(Oh. ___

*Two gtrs. arr. for one.

**Applies to Bkgd. Voc. only.

Voc. Fill 1

Gtr. 3: w/ Rhy. Fig. 3 (7 times)
3rd time, Gtr. 6: w/ Riff D (6 1/2 times)

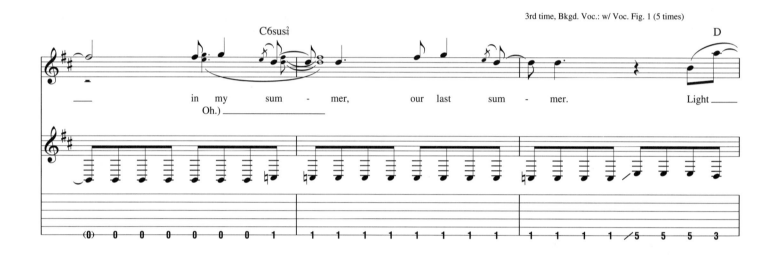

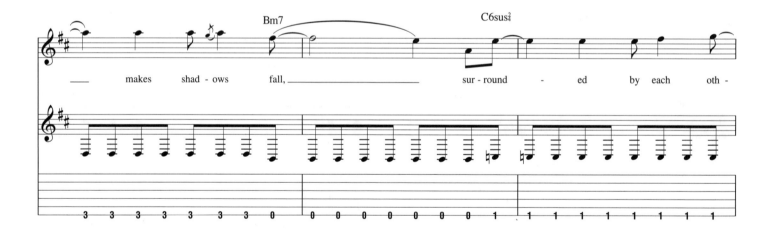

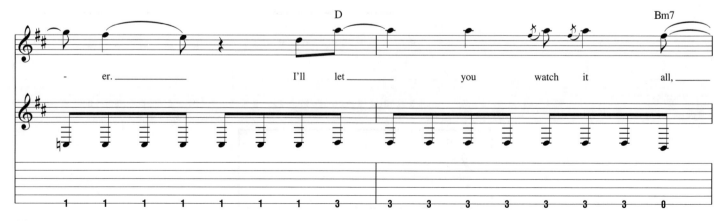

C6sus²₄

N.C.

a view ___ from our last sum - mer. _____

Interlude

Gtr. 1: w/ Riff A (4 times)
Gtr. 2: w/ Rhy. Fig. 1
Gtr. 5 tacet

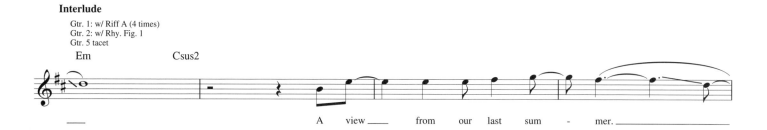

Em   Csus2

___   A   view ___ from   our   last   sum - mer. _____

Em   Csus2

Verse

Gtr. 2: w/ Riff B (1 3/4 times)

Csus2   G/B   D   Dsus4

2. We trace the sun ___ a - cross ___ the sky...

(And we laugh ___ till we ___ cry. ___

Gtr. 1

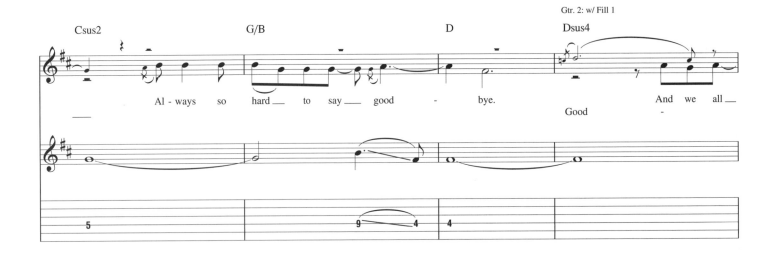

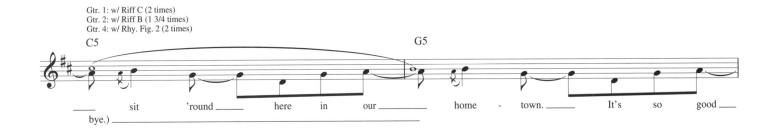

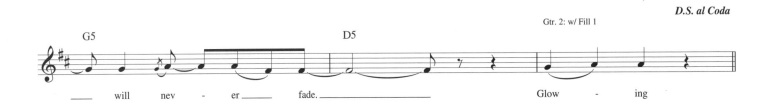

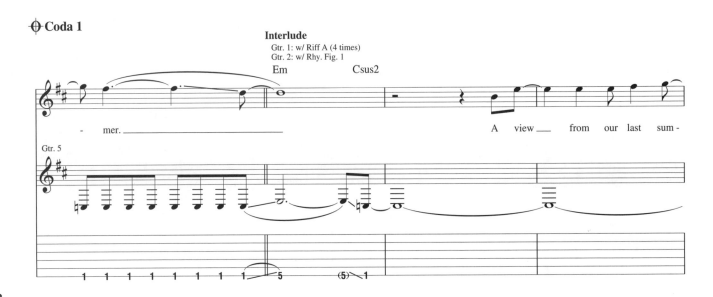

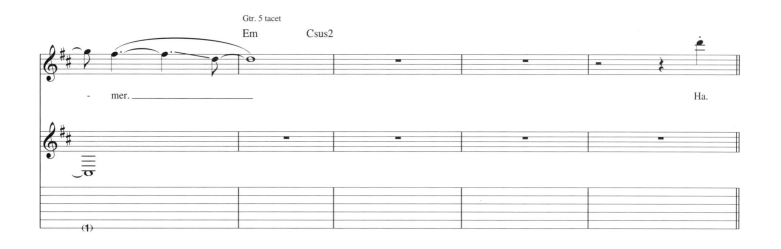

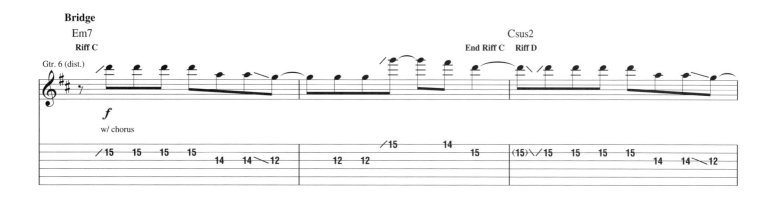

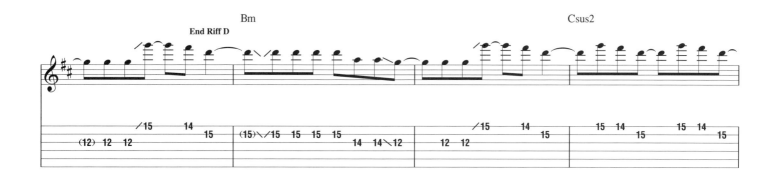

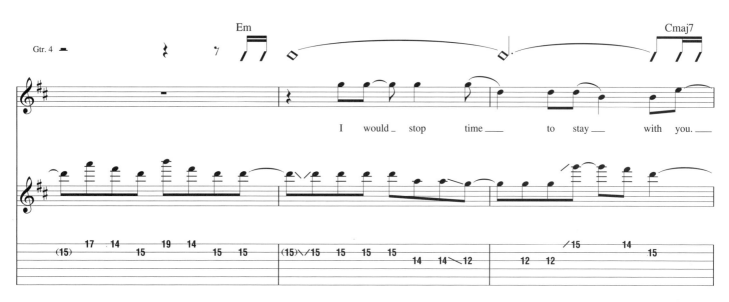

I would __ stop time __ so we __ don't __ move. __ I would __ stop time. __

D.S.S. al Coda 2

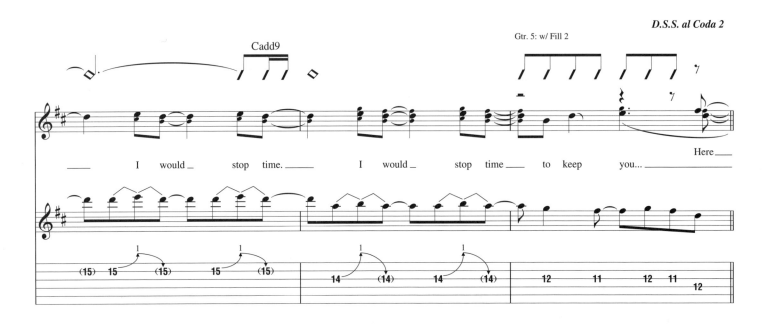

Cadd9

Gtr. 5: w/ Fill 2

I would __ stop time. __ I would __ stop time __ to keep __ you... __

Here __

✦ **Coda 2**

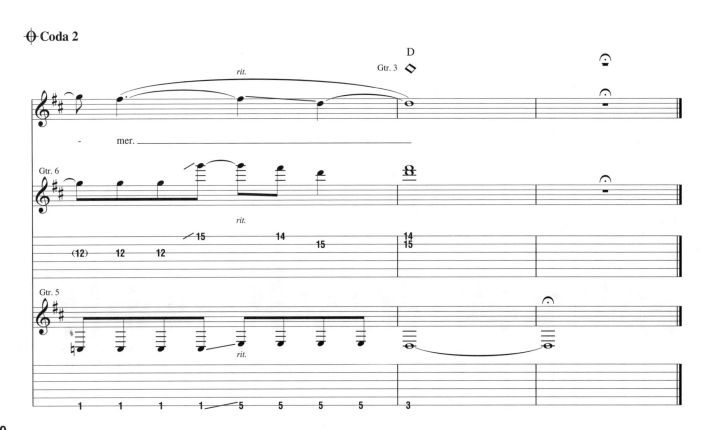

- mer. __

Gtr. 3

D

Gtr. 6

rit.

rit.

Gtr. 5

rit.

Sway

Words and Music by Michael Lewis, Ian Watkins, Richard Oliver, Lee Gaze, Stuart Richardson and Michael Chiplin

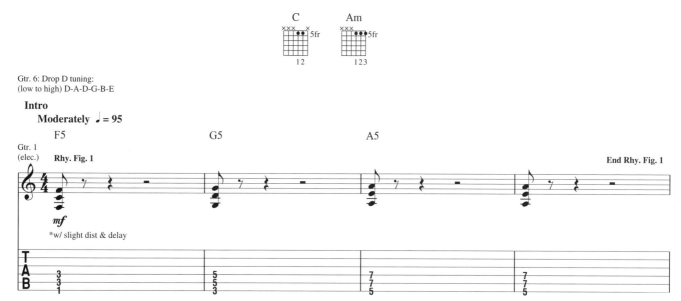

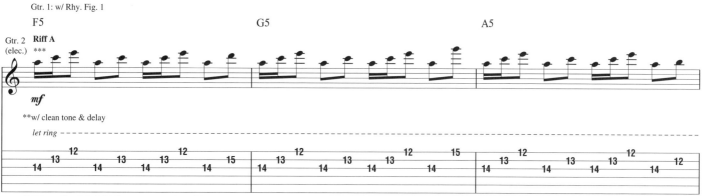

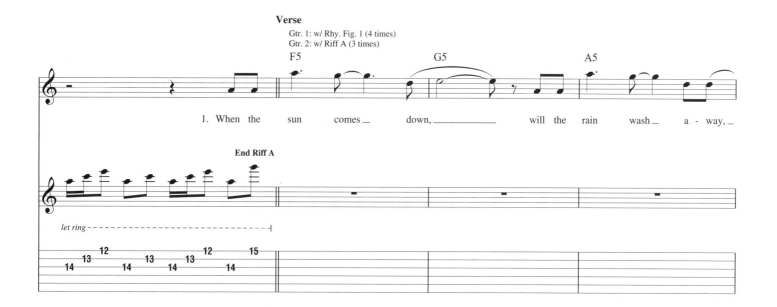

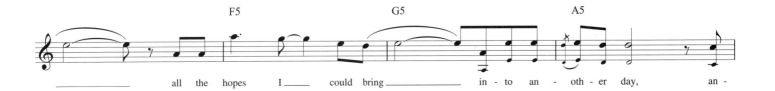

all the hopes I___ could bring_____ in - to an - oth - er day, an -

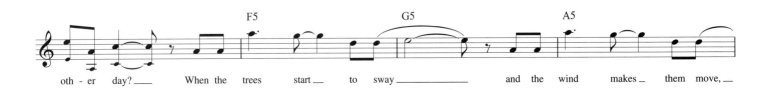

oth - er day? ___ When the trees start ___ to sway _____ and the wind makes ___ them move, ___

_____ I can tell ___ that you don't _____ know. _____

𝄋 Pre-Chorus

2nd time, Gtr. 4: w/ Rhy. Fig. 3

___ To all _____ the fights I've con - quered and ___ be - yond. ___

Rhy. Fig. 2

*Gtr. 3

mf

*Elec. piano arr. for gtr.

Gtr. 3: w/ Rhy. Fig. 2 (3 times)

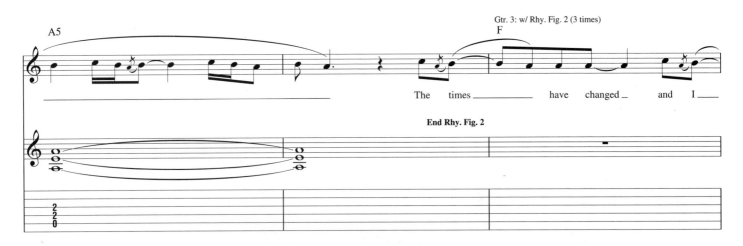

_____ The times _____ have changed ___ and I

End Rhy. Fig. 2

_____ will now move o - ver slow - ly. _____ Though true ___

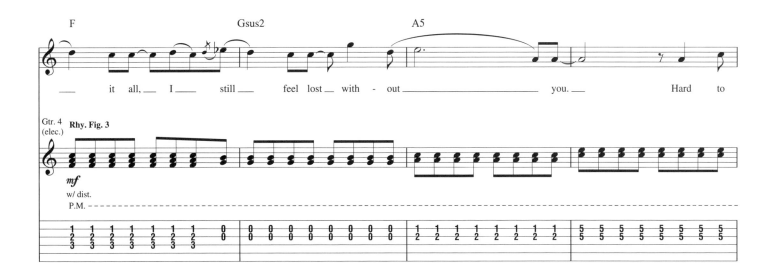

it all, ___ I ___ still ___ feel lost ___ with - out _____ you. ___ Hard to

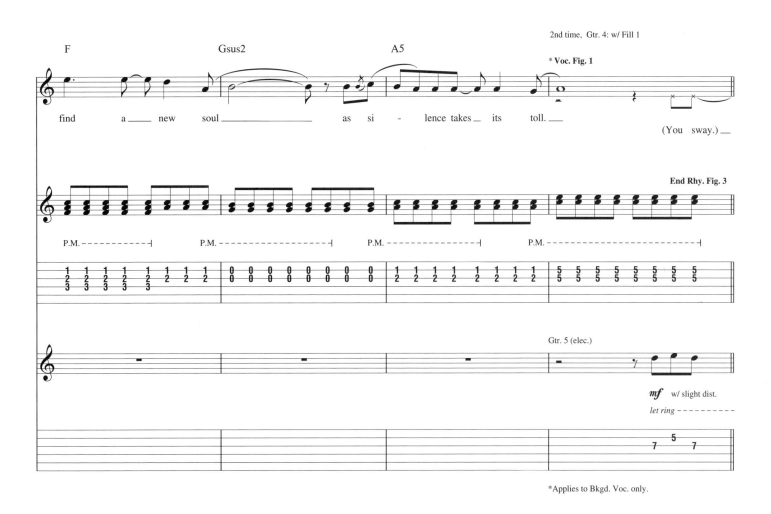

find a ___ new soul _____ as si - lence takes ___ its toll. ___

(You sway.) ___

*Applies to Bkgd. Voc. only.

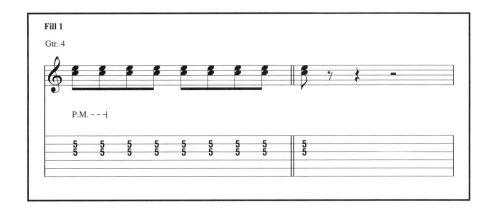

Chorus

Gtr. 4 tacet

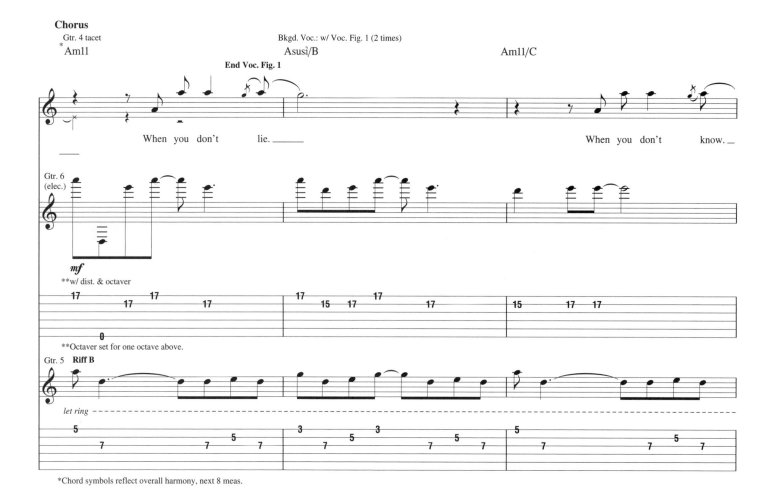

*Chord symbols reflect overall harmony, next 8 meas.

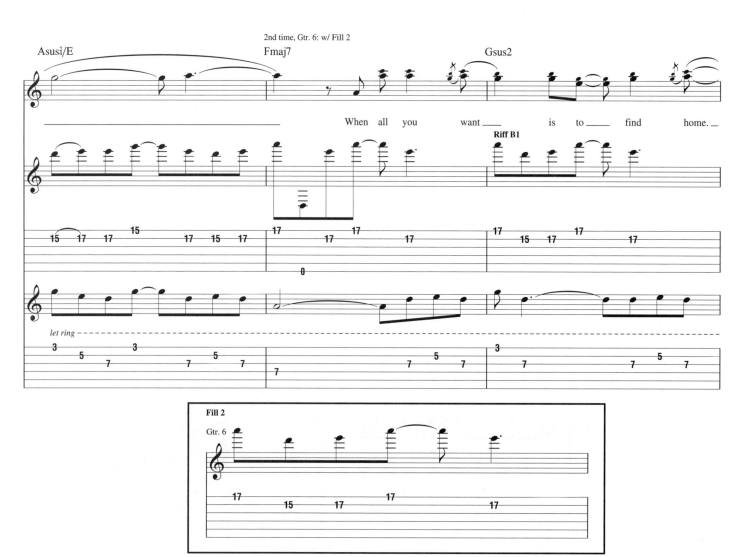

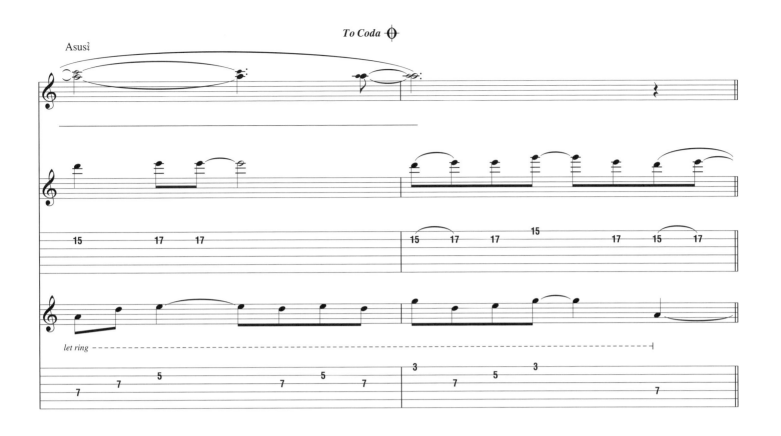

Interlude

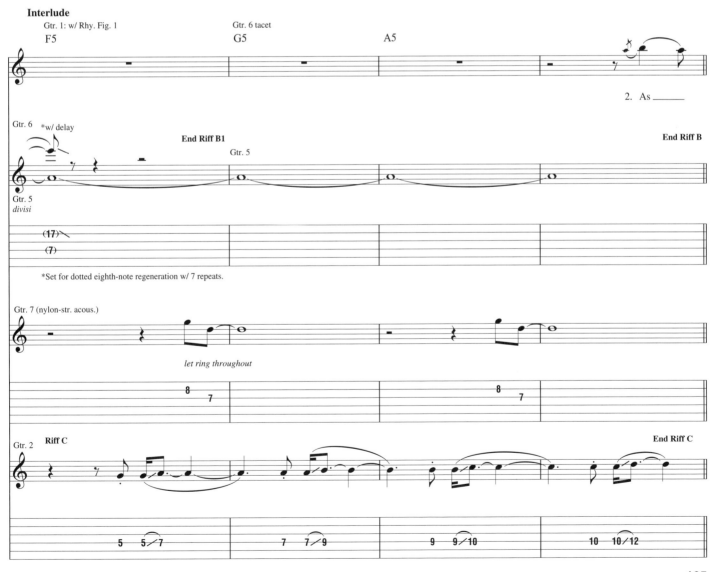

Verse

Gtr. 1: w/ Rhy. Fig. 1 (3 times)
Gtrs. 5 & 7 tacet

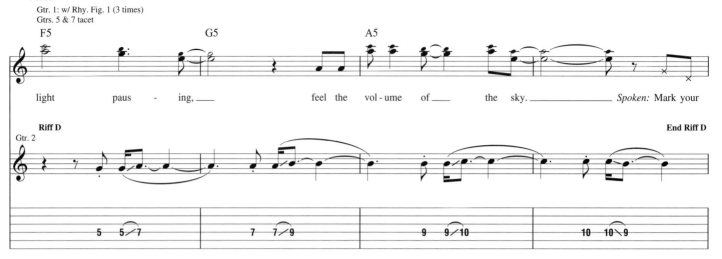

light   paus - ing, ___   feel the   vol - ume   of ___   the   sky. ___   *Spoken:* Mark your

Gtr. 2: w/ Riff C (2 times)

place   in   time ___   with an - oth - er ___   ques - tion   why. ___   Ti - ny

flick - ers   in ___   the   night ___   al - ways   look - ing   to ___   be ___   right. ___   To   all ___

Coda

Bkgd. Voc.: w/ Voc. Fig. 1 (3 times)

Gtr. 5: w/ Riff B

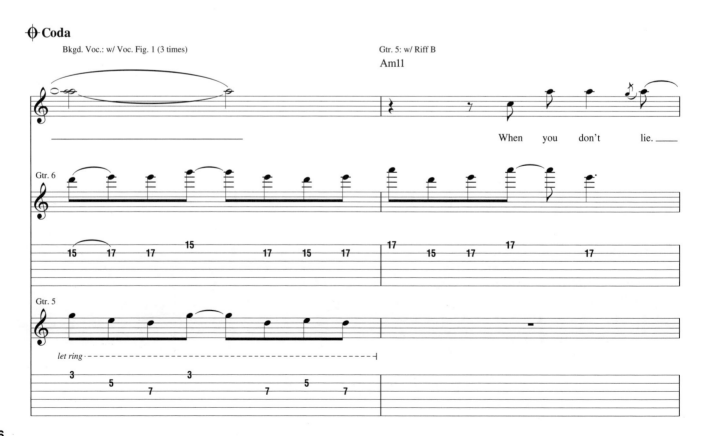

When   you   don't   lie. ___

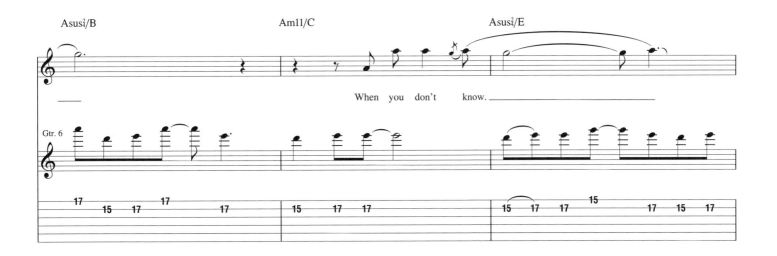

When you don't know.

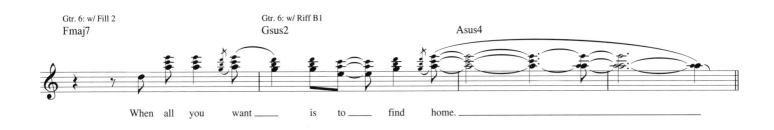

When all you want ___ is to ___ find home. ___

Outro

Oh, ___ oh, ___ oh, ___

*Gtr. 8 (elec.) w/ dist., *mf*

oh. ___ Oh, ___ oh, ___

Guitar Notation Legend

Guitar Music can be notated three different ways: on a *musical staff*, in *tablature*, and in *rhythm slashes*.

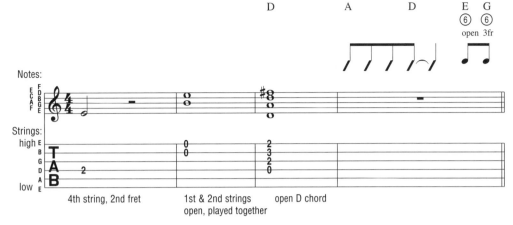

RHYTHM SLASHES are written above the staff. Strum chords in the rhythm indicated. Use the chord diagrams found at the top of the first page of the transcription for the appropriate chord voicings. Round noteheads indicate single notes.

THE MUSICAL STAFF shows pitches and rhythms and is divided by bar lines into measures. Pitches are named after the first seven letters of the alphabet.

TABLATURE graphically represents the guitar fingerboard. Each horizontal line represents a a string, and each number represents a fret.

4th string, 2nd fret

1st & 2nd strings open, played together

open D chord

Definitions for Special Guitar Notation

HALF-STEP BEND: Strike the note and bend up 1/2 step.

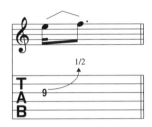

WHOLE-STEP BEND: Strike the note and bend up one step.

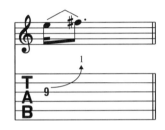

GRACE NOTE BEND: Strike the note and immediately bend up as indicated.

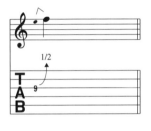

SLIGHT (MICROTONE) BEND: Strike the note and bend up 1/4 step.

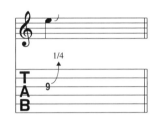

BEND AND RELEASE: Strike the note and bend up as indicated, then release back to the original note. Only the first note is struck.

PRE-BEND: Bend the note as indicated, then strike it.

PRE-BEND AND RELEASE: Bend the note as indicated. Strike it and release the bend back to the original note.

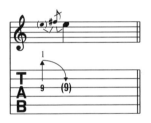

UNISON BEND: Strike the two notes simultaneously and bend the lower note up to the pitch of the higher.

VIBRATO: The string is vibrated by rapidly bending and releasing the note with the fretting hand.

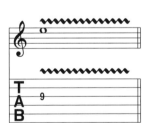

WIDE VIBRATO: The pitch is varied to a greater degree by vibrating with the fretting hand.

HAMMER-ON: Strike the first (lower) note with one finger, then sound the higher note (on the same string) with another finger by fretting it without picking.

PULL-OFF: Place both fingers on the notes to be sounded. Strike the first note and without picking, pull the finger off to sound the second (lower) note.

LEGATO SLIDE: Strike the first note and then slide the same fret-hand finger up or down to the second note. The second note is not struck.

SHIFT SLIDE: Same as legato slide, except the second note is struck.

TRILL: Very rapidly alternate between the notes indicated by continuously hammering on and pulling off.

TAPPING: Hammer ("tap") the fret indicated with the pick-hand index or middle finger and pull off to the note fretted by the fret hand.

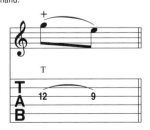

NATURAL HARMONIC: Strike the note while the fret-hand lightly touches the string directly over the fret indicated.

PINCH HARMONIC: The note is fretted normally and a harmonic is produced by adding the edge of the thumb or the tip of the index finger of the pick hand to the normal pick attack.

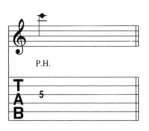

HARP HARMONIC: The note is fretted normally and a harmonic is produced by gently resting the pick hand's index finger directly above the indicated fret (in parentheses) while the pick hand's thumb or pick assists by plucking the appropriate string.

PICK SCRAPE: The edge of the pick is rubbed down (or up) the string, producing a scratchy sound.

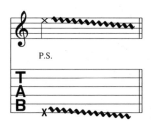

MUFFLED STRINGS: A percussive sound is produced by laying the fret hand across the string(s) without depressing, and striking them with the pick hand.

PALM MUTING: The note is partially muted by the pick hand lightly touching the string(s) just before the bridge.

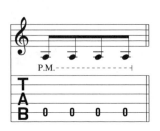

RAKE: Drag the pick across the strings indicated with a single motion.

TREMOLO PICKING: The note is picked as rapidly and continuously as possible.

ARPEGGIATE: Play the notes of the chord indicated by quickly rolling them from bottom to top.

VIBRATO BAR DIVE AND RETURN: The pitch of the note or chord is dropped a specified number of steps (in rhythm) then returned to the original pitch.

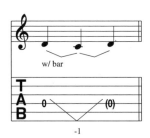

VIBRATO BAR SCOOP: Depress the bar just before striking the note, then quickly release the bar.

VIBRATO BAR DIP: Strike the note and then immediately drop a specified number of steps, then release back to the original pitch.

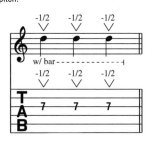

Additional Musical Definitions

>	(accent)	• Accentuate note (play it louder)
∧	(accent)	• Accentuate note with great intensity
•	(staccato)	• Play the note short
⊓		• Downstroke
∨		• Upstroke
D.S. al Coda		• Go back to the sign (𝄋), then play until the measure marked "**To Coda**," then skip to the section labelled "**Coda**."
D.C. al Fine		• Go back to the beginning of the song and play until the measure marked "**Fine**" (end).

Rhy. Fig.	• Label used to recall a recurring accompaniment pattern (usually chordal).
Riff	• Label used to recall composed, melodic lines (usually single notes) which recur.
Fill	• Label used to identify a brief melodic figure which is to be inserted into the arrangement.
Rhy. Fill	• A chordal version of a Fill.
tacet	• Instrument is silent (drops out).

• Repeat measures between signs.

• When a repeated section has different endings, play the first ending only the first time and the second ending only the second time.

NOTE: Tablature numbers in parentheses mean:
1. The note is being sustained over a system (note in standard notation is tied), or
2. The note is sustained, but a new articulation (such as a hammer-on, pull-off, slide or vibrato begins), or
3. The note is a barely audible "ghost" note (note in standard notation is also in parentheses).

RECORDED VERSIONS
The Best Note-For-Note Transcriptions Available

ALL BOOKS INCLUDE TABLATURE

00690501	Adams, Bryan – Greatest Hits	$19.95
00692015	Aerosmith – Greatest Hits	$22.95
00690178	Alice in Chains – Acoustic	$19.95
00690387	Alice in Chains – Nothing Safe: The Best of the Box	$19.95
00694932	Allman Brothers Band – Volume 1	$24.95
00694933	Allman Brothers Band – Volume 2	$24.95
00694878	Atkins, Chet – Vintage Fingerstyle	$19.95
00690418	Audio Adrenaline, Best of	$17.95
00690609	Audioslave	$19.95
00690366	Bad Company – Original Anthology, Book 1	$19.95
00690503	Beach Boys – Very Best of	$19.95
00690489	Beatles – 1	$24.95
00694929	Beatles – 1962-1966	$24.95
00694930	Beatles – 1967-1970	$24.95
00694832	Beatles – For Acoustic Guitar	$19.95
00690137	Beatles – A Hard Day's Night	$16.95
00690482	Beatles – Let It Be	$16.95
00690632	Beck – Sea Change	$19.95
00694884	Benson, George – Best of	$19.95
00692385	Berry, Chuck	$19.95
00692200	Black Sabbath – We Sold Our Soul for Rock 'N' Roll	$19.95
00690674	Blink-182	$19.95
00690389	Blink-182 – Enema of the State	$19.95
00690523	Blink-182 – Take Off Your Pants & Jacket	$19.95
00690028	Blue Oyster Cult – Cult Classics	$19.95
00690583	Boxcar Racer	$19.95
00690491	Bowie, David – Best of	$19.95
00690451	Buckley, Jeff – Collection	$24.95
00690364	Cake – Songbook	$19.95
00690564	Calling, The – Camino Palmero	$29.95
00690043	Cheap Trick – Best of	$19.95
00690567	Christian, Charlie – Definitive Collection	$19.95
00690590	Clapton, Eric – Anthology	$29.95
00692391	Clapton, Eric – Best of, 2nd Edition	$22.95
00690415	Clapton Chronicles – Best of Eric Clapton	$18.95
00690074	Clapton, Eric – The Cream of Clapton	$24.95
00694869	Clapton, Eric – Unplugged	$22.95
00690162	Clash, Best of The	$19.95
00690494	Coldplay – Parachutes	$19.95
00690593	Coldplay – A Rush of Blood to the Head	$19.95
00694940	Counting Crows – August & Everything After	$19.95
00690401	Creed – Human Clay	$19.95
00690352	Creed – My Own Prison	$19.95
00690551	Creed – Weathered	$19.95
00699521	Cure, The – Greatest Hits	$24.95
00690484	dc Talk – Intermission: The Greatest Hits	$19.95
00690289	Deep Purple, Best of	$17.95
00690563	Default – The Fallout	$19.95
00690384	Di Franco, Ani – Best of	$19.95
00695382	Dire Straits – Sultans of Swing	$19.95
00690347	Doors, The – Anthology	$22.95
00690348	Doors, The – Essential Guitar Collection	$16.95
00690555	Etheridge, Melissa – Best of	$19.95
00690524	Etheridge, Melissa – Skin	$19.95
00690515	Extreme II – Pornograffitti	$19.95
00690235	Foo Fighters – The Colour and the Shape	$19.95
00690595	Foo Fighters – One by One	$19.95
00690394	Foo Fighters – There Is Nothing Left to Lose	$19.95
00690222	G3 Live – Satriani, Vai, Johnson	$22.95
00690338	Goo Goo Dolls – Dizzy Up the Girl	$19.95
00690576	Goo Goo Dolls – Gutterflower	$19.95

00690601	Good Charlotte – The Young and the Hopeless	$19.95
00690591	Griffin, Patty – Guitar Collection	$19.95
00694798	Harrison, George – Anthology	$19.95
00692930	Hendrix, Jimi – Are You Experienced?	$24.95
00692931	Hendrix, Jimi – Axis: Bold As Love	$22.95
00690017	Hendrix, Jimi – Live at Woodstock	$24.95
00690602	Hendrix, Jimi – Smash Hits	$19.95
00660029	Holly, Buddy	$19.95
00690457	Incubus – Make Yourself	$19.95
00690544	Incubus – Morningview	$19.95
00690136	Indigo Girls – 1200 Curfews	$22.95
00694912	Johnson, Eric – Ah Via Musicom	$19.95
00690660	Johnson, Eric – Best of	$19.95
00690271	Johnson, Robert – New Transcriptions	$24.95
00699131	Joplin, Janis – Best of	$19.95
00690427	Judas Priest – Best of	$19.95
00690504	King, Albert – The Very Best of	$19.95
00690444	King, B.B. and Eric Clapton – Riding with the King	$19.95
00690339	Kinks, The – Best of	$19.95
00690614	Lavigne, Avril – Let Go	$19.95
00690525	Lynch, George – Best of	$19.95
00694755	Malmsteen, Yngwie – Rising Force	$19.95
00694956	Marley, Bob – Legend	$19.95
00690548	Marley, Bob – One Love: Very Best of	$19.95
00694945	Marley, Bob – Songs of Freedom	$24.95
00690616	Matchbox 20 – More Than You Think You Are	$19.95
00690239	Matchbox 20 – Yourself or Someone Like You	$19.95
00690382	McLachlan, Sarah – Mirrorball	$19.95
00694952	Megadeth – Countdown to Extinction	$19.95
00694951	Megadeth – Rust in Peace	$22.95
00690495	Megadeth – The World Needs a Hero	$19.95
00690505	Mellencamp, John – Guitar Collection	$19.95
00690562	Metheny, Pat – Bright Size Life	$19.95
00690559	Metheny, Pat – Question and Answer	$19.95
00690611	Nirvana	$22.95
00690189	Nirvana – From the Muddy Banks of the Wishkah	$19.95
00694913	Nirvana – In Utero	$19.95
00694883	Nirvana – Nevermind	$19.95
00690026	Nirvana – Unplugged in New York	$19.95
00690121	Oasis – (What's the Story) Morning Glory	$19.95
00690358	Offspring, The – Americana	$19.95
00690485	Offspring, The – Conspiracy of One	$19.95
00690552	Offspring, The – Ignition	$19.95
00690663	Offspring, The – Splinter	$19.95
00694847	Osbourne, Ozzy – Best of	$22.95
00690547	Osbourne, Ozzy – Down to Earth	$19.95
00690399	Osbourne, Ozzy – Ozzman Cometh	$19.95
00694855	Pearl Jam – Ten	$19.95
00690439	Perfect Circle, A – Mer De Noms	$19.95
00690499	Petty, Tom – The Definitive Guitar Collection	$19.95
00690424	Phish – Farmhouse	$19.95
00690240	Phish – Hoist	$19.95
00690607	Phish – Round Room	$19.95
00690331	Phish – Story of the Ghost	$19.95
00690642	Pillar – Fireproof	$19.95
00690428	Pink Floyd – Dark Side of the Moon	$19.95
00690546	P.O.D. – Satellite	$19.95
00693864	Police, The – Best of	$19.95
00690299	Presley, Elvis – Best of Elvis: The King of Rock 'n' Roll	$19.95
00694975	Queen – Greatest Hits	$24.95
00694910	Rage Against the Machine	$19.95

00690145	Rage Against the Machine – Evil Empire	$19.95
00690426	Ratt – Best of	$19.95
00690055	Red Hot Chili Peppers – Bloodsugarsexmagik	$19.95
00690584	Red Hot Chili Peppers – By the Way	$19.95
00690379	Red Hot Chili Peppers – Californication	$19.95
00690090	Red Hot Chili Peppers – One Hot Minute	$22.95
00690511	Reinhardt, Django – Definitive Collection	$19.95
00690643	Relient K – Two Lefts Don't Make a Right...But Three Do	$19.95
00690014	Rolling Stones – Exile on Main Street	$24.95
00690631	Rolling Stones – Guitar Anthology	$24.95
00690600	Saliva – Back Into Your System	$19.95
00690031	Santana's Greatest Hits	$19.95
00690566	Scorpions – Best of	$19.95
00690604	Seger, Bob – Guitar Collection	$19.95
00690419	Slipknot	$19.95
00690530	Slipknot – Iowa	$19.95
00690385	Sonicflood	$19.95
00690021	Sting – Fields of Gold	$19.95
00690597	Stone Sour	$19.95
00690520	Styx Guitar Collection	$19.95
00690519	Sum 41 – All Killer No Filler	$19.95
00690612	Sum 41 – Does This Look Infected?	$19.95
00690425	System of a Down	$19.95
00690606	System of a Down – Steal This Album	$19.95
00690531	System of a Down – Toxicity	$19.95
00694824	Taylor, James – Best of	$16.95
00690238	Third Eye Blind	$19.95
00690580	311 – From Chaos	$19.95
00690295	Tool – Aenima	$19.95
00690654	Train – Best of	$19.95
00690039	Vai, Steve – Alien Love Secrets	$24.95
00690392	Vai, Steve – The Ultra Zone	$19.95
00690370	Vaughan, Stevie Ray and Double Trouble – The Real Deal: Greatest Hits Volume 2	$22.95
00690116	Vaughan, Stevie Ray – Guitar Collection	$24.95
00660058	Vaughan, Stevie Ray – Lightnin' Blues 1983-1987	$24.95
00690550	Vaughan, Stevie Ray and Double Trouble – Live at Montreux 1982 & 1985	$24.95
00694835	Vaughan, Stevie Ray – The Sky Is Crying	$22.95
00690015	Vaughan, Stevie Ray – Texas Flood	$19.95
00694789	Waters, Muddy – Deep Blues	$24.95
00690071	Weezer (The Blue Album)	$19.95
00690516	Weezer (The Green Album)	$19.95
00690579	Weezer – Maladroit	$19.95
00690286	Weezer – Pinkerton	$19.95
00690447	Who, The – Best of	$24.95
00690640	Wilcox, David – Anthology 2000-2003	$19.95
00690320	Williams, Dar – Best of	$17.95
00690596	Yardbirds, The – Best of	$19.95
00690443	Zappa, Frank – Hot Rats	$19.95
00690589	ZZ Top Guitar Anthology	$22.95

GUITAR PLAY-ALONG

INCLUDES TAB

This series will help you play your favorite songs quickly and easily. Just follow the tab and listen to the CD to hear how the guitar should sound, and then play along using the separate backing tracks. Mac or PC users can also slow down the tempo by using the CD in their computer. The melody and lyrics are also included in the book so that you can sing or simply follow along.

VOL. 1 – ROCK GUITAR
00699570 / $12.95

Day Tripper • Message in a Bottle • Refugee • Shattered • Sunshine of Your Love • Takin' Care of Business • Tush • Walk This Way.

VOL. 2 – ACOUSTIC
00699569 / $12.95

Angie • Behind Blue Eyes • Best of My Love • Blackbird • Dust in the Wind • Layla • Night Moves • Yesterday.

VOL. 3 – HARD ROCK
00699573 / $14.95

Crazy Train • Iron Man • Living After Midnight • Rock You Like a Hurricane • Round and Round • Smoke on the Water • Sweet Child O' Mine • You Really Got Me.

VOL. 4 – POP/ROCK
00699571 / $12.95

Breakdown • Crazy Little Thing Called Love • Hit Me with Your Best Shot • I Want You to Want Me • Lights • R.O.C.K. in the U.S.A. (A Salute to 60's Rock) • Summer of '69 • What I Like About You.

VOL. 5 – MODERN ROCK
00699574 / $12.95

Aerials • Alive • Bother • Chop Suey! • Control • Last Resort • Take a Look Around (Theme from "M:I-2") • Wish You Were Here.

VOL. 6 – '90S ROCK
00699572 / $12.95

Are You Gonna Go My Way • Come Out and Play • I'll Stick Around • Know Your Enemy • Man in the Box • Outshined • Smells Like Teen Spirit • Under the Bridge.

VOL. 7 – BLUES GUITAR
00699575 / $12.95

All Your Love (I Miss Loving) • Born Under a Bad Sign • Hide Away • I'm Tore Down • I'm Your Hoochie Coochie Man • Pride and Joy • Sweet Home Chicago • The Thrill Is Gone.

VOL. 8 – ROCK
00699585 / $12.95

All Right Now • Black Magic Woman • Get Back • Hey Joe • Layla • Love Me Two Times • Won't Get Fooled Again • You Really Got Me.

VOL. 9 – PUNK ROCK
00699576 / $12.95

All the Small Things • Fat Lip • Flavor of the Weak • I Feel So • Lifestyles of the Rich and Famous • (So) Tired of Waiting for You • Say It Ain't So • Self Esteem.

VOL. 10 – ACOUSTIC
00699586 / $12.95

Here Comes the Sun • Landslide • The Magic Bus • Norwegian Wood (This Bird Has Flown) • Pink Houses • Space Oddity • Tangled Up in Blue • Tears in Heaven.

VOL. 11 – EARLY ROCK
00699579 / $12.95

Fun, Fun, Fun • Hound Dog • Louie, Louie • No Particular Place to Go • Oh, Pretty Woman • Rock Around the Clock • Under the Boardwalk • Wild Thing.

VOL. 12 – POP/ROCK
00699587 / $12.95

867-5309/Jenny • Every Breath You Take • Money for Nothing • Rebel, Rebel • Run to You • Ticket to Ride • Wonderful Tonight • You Give Love a Bad Name.

VOL. 13 – FOLK ROCK
00699581 / $12.95

Annie's Song • Leaving on a Jet Plane • Suite: Judy Blue Eyes • This Land Is Your Land • Time in a Bottle • Turn! Turn! Turn! (To Everything There Is a Season) • You've Got a Friend • You've Got to Hide Your Love Away.

VOL. 14 – BLUES ROCK
00699582 / $14.95

Blue on Black • Crossfire • Cross Road Blues (Crossroads) • The House Is Rockin' • La Grange • Move It on Over • Roadhouse Blues • Statesboro Blues.

VOL. 15 – R&B
00699583 / $12.95

Ain't Too Proud to Beg • Brick House • Get Ready • I Can't Help Myself (Sugar Pie, Honey Bunch) • I Got You (I Feel Good) • I Heard It Through the Grapevine • My Girl • Shining Star.

VOL. 16 – JAZZ
00699584 / $12.95

All Blues • Bluesette • Footprints • How Insensitive (Insensatez) • Misty • Satin Doll • Stella by Starlight • Tenor Madness.

VOL. 17 – COUNTRY
00699588 / $12.95

Amie • Boot Scootin' Boogie • Chattahoochee • Folsom Prison Blues • Friends in Low Places • Forever and Ever, Amen • T-R-O-U-B-L-E • Workin' Man Blues.

VOL. 18 – ACOUSTIC ROCK
00699577 / $14.95

About a Girl • Breaking the Girl • Drive • Iris • More Than Words • Patience • Silent Lucidity • 3 AM.

VOL. 19 – SOUL
00699578 / $12.95

Get Up (I Feel Like Being) a Sex Machine • Green Onions • In the Midnight Hour • Knock on Wood • Mustang Sally • Respect • (Sittin' On) the Dock of the Bay • Soul Man.

VOL. 20 – ROCKABILLY
00699580 / $12.95

Be-Bop-A-Lula • Blue Suede Shoes • Hello Mary Lou • Little Sister • Mystery Train • Rock This Town • Stray Cat Strut • That'll Be the Day.

VOL. 21 – YULETIDE
00699602 / $12.95

Angels We Have Heard on High • Away in a Manger • Deck the Hall • The First Noel • Go, Tell It on the Mountain • Jingle Bells • Joy to the World • O Little Town of Bethlehem.

VOL. 22 – CHRISTMAS
00699600 / $12.95

The Christmas Song (Chestnuts Roasting on an Open Fire) • Frosty the Snow Man • Happy Xmas (War Is Over) • Here Comes Santa Claus (Right Down Santa Claus Lane) • Jingle-Bell Rock • Merry Christmas, Darling • Rudolph the Red-Nosed Reindeer • Silver Bells.

VOL. 23 – SURF
00699635 / $12.95

Let's Go Trippin' • Out of Limits • Penetration • Pipeline • Surf City • Surfin' U.S.A. • Walk Don't Run • The Wedge.

VOL. 24 – ERIC CLAPTON
00699649 / $14.95

Badge • Bell Bottom Blues • Change the World • Cocaine • Key to the Highway • Lay Down Sally • White Room • Wonderful Tonight.

VOL. 25 – LENNON AND MCCARTNEY
00699642 / $14.95

Back in the U.S.S.R. • Drive My Car • Get Back • A Hard Day's Night • I Feel Fine • Paperback Writer • Revolution • Ticket to Ride.

VOL. 26 – ELVIS PRESLEY
00699643 / $14.95

All Shook Up • Blue Suede Shoes • Don't Be Cruel (To a Heart That's True) • Heartbreak Hotel • Hound Dog • Jailhouse Rock • Little Sister • Mystery Train.

VOL. 27 – DAVID LEE ROTH
00699645 / $14.95

Ain't Talkin' 'Bout Love • Dance the Night Away • Just Like Paradise • A Lil' Ain't Enough • Panama • Runnin' with the Devil • Unchained • Yankee Rose.

VOL. 28 – GREG KOCH
00699646 / $14.95

Chief's Blues • Death of a Bassman • Dylan the Villain • The Grip • Holy Grail • Spank It • Tonus Diabolicus • Zoiks.

VOL. 29 – BOB SEGER
00699647 / $14.95

Against the Wind • Betty Lou's Gettin' Out Tonight • Hollywood Nights • Mainstreet • Night Moves • Old Time Rock & Roll • Rock and Roll Never Forgets • Still the Same.

VOL. 30 – KISS
00699644 / $14.95

Cold Gin • Detroit Rock City • Deuce • Firehouse • Heaven's on Fire • Love Gun • Rock and Roll All Nite • Shock Me.

VOL. 31 – CHRISTMAS HITS
00699652 / $12.95

Blue Christmas • Do You Hear What I Hear • Happy Holiday • I Saw Mommy Kissing Santa Claus • I'll Be Home for Christmas • Let It Snow! Let It Snow! Let It Snow! • Little Saint Nick • Snowfall.

Prices, contents, and availability subject to change without notice.

FOR MORE INFORMATION, SEE YOUR LOCAL MUSIC DEALER, OR WRITE TO:

HAL•LEONARD®
CORPORATION

7777 W. BLUEMOUND RD. P.O. BOX 13819 MILWAUKEE, WI 53213

Visit Hal Leonard online at www.halleonard.com

0604